FEB

Analyzing Jobs and Tasks

Techniques in
Training and Performance Development
Series

Analyzing Jobs and Tasks

Kenneth E. Carlisle

Series Editor
Joseph W. Arwady

Educational Technology Publications
Englewood Cliffs, New Jersey 07632

Library of Congress Cataloging-in-Publication Data

Carlisle, Kenneth Eugene, 1949-
  Analyzing jobs and tasks.

  (Techniques in training and performance development series)
  Bibliography: p.
  Includes index.
  1. Job analysis. I. Title. II. Series.
HF5549.5.J6C36   1986   658.3'06   85-20661
ISBN 0-87778-194-X

Printed in the United States of America.

Library of Congress Catalog Card Number: 85-20661.

International Standard Book Number: 0-87778-194-X.

First Printing: January, 1986.

Acknowledgments

Many people have influenced the creation of this book. However, the author would like to specifically express thanks to two individuals:

- **Dr. Ivor K. Davies**, whose inspired teaching and direction defined the process of analysis upon which this book is based.

- **Mr. James W. Engbarth**, whose critical and patient editing of this and other work greatly influenced the author's writing.

Editor's Preface

In *Analyzing Jobs and Tasks*, Kenneth E. Carlisle has compressed fifteen years of research, analysis, and application into thirty-three techniques. Each is designed to achieve a single objective: equip the reader with a practical tool to use in a real performance-improvement effort. And, here, Carlisle is at his best, dissecting the stages of analysis in the broad context of the real world of work, where analysts must do more than analyze—they must also *do*.

As an author, Carlisle doesn't offer advice on the run. He doesn't trip us up with empty expressions and alien jargon. He doesn't try to sell a quick fix, even when we want to buy one. Instead, he continues to refine our understanding of the relationships between the structure of work and human productivity. Fortunately, this focus on substance makes him ideally suited for the *TECHNIQUES IN TRAINING AND PERFORMANCE DEVELOPMENT* series.

As you scan the Table of Contents and then the individual techniques, note the exacting style and step-by-step explanations. Once you've read through two or three techniques, you may feel as I do—the perspective is so embedded in the roll-up-your-sleeves world of work that *using* the techniques is almost unavoidable. Carlisle has been there many times, working to solve difficult performance problems and producing measurable results. Clearly, *Analyzing Jobs and Tasks* is a book written *for* practitioners *by* a practitioner.

That's equally true for every book in the series. Collectively, they provide the practitioner with an inventory of approximately 400 techniques, each purposefully selected, formatted, and written to improve performance in the workplace. I believe the series will prove to be the most useful resource ever made available to training and performance professionals.

For his part, Ken Carlisle has done his job well and, I might add, on schedule. In the world of publishing, meeting deadlines for a single manuscript (let alone a series of ten) is most uncommon. I suppose that says something else about Carlisle's ideas about work.

Joseph W. Arwady
Series Editor
October 1985

Table of Contents

Analyzing Jobs and Tasks

1

Getting Ready to Analyze the Job

This book is about the analysis of human performance. It might be titled job analysis, task analysis, or work analysis. Unfortunately, these titles have become confused by a variety of limiting definitions and techniques. Recently, for example, a consulting company was contracted to do a task analysis of the control room operation at a nuclear power plant. A team of consultants arrived to perform the analysis. They videotaped the operators at work, interviewed them to fill in work details, produced long lists of tasks and equipment, and revised the lists from operator input. The result was a long, detailed list of what the operators did. The list was acclaimed as a well-done task analysis. It was then filed in the training department library, and never read again.

Had a task analysis been done? Yes and no. A technique of analysis had been used to describe what operators did when following set operating procedures. But the results did not meet an actual need. They simply verified procedures which already described the task in detail. Was some form of analysis required? Sure. Many new procedures could have been written. Perhaps the videotapes could have been developed into training materials. But the analysts' insistance that they knew how to do a task analysis limited their horizons. In effect, they were seeking problems on which to graft their solution.

Another example is a task analysis performed in the hospitality industry. This time the analysts spent several months analyzing basic jobs in hotels and developing job aids—basic lists of task steps with related pictures and scripts of things to say while working. The job aids resulted in improved performance in many areas of the hotel, such as the front desk and restaurant. The housekeeping department, however, was not using them. The reason was immediately evident when housekeepers were interviewed. Most maids could not read well. Many spoke very little English. They did not learn well from written directions; they required visual demonstration and practice to improve their performance. Again the analysts failed to consider the special needs of the work place, and let their technique of task analysis and written job aids limit the analysis results.

These examples illustrate several problems common to the analysis of jobs and tasks. First, the lack of uniform analysis terminology made communication very difficult between the various analysts and those needing the analysis. The task analysis performed for nuclear power operators produced very different results than the task analysis performed for the hotel industry. Yet both sets of analysts called their technique task analysis.

A lack of uniform terminology leads to a second, more serious problem. Each analyst learns one analysis technique which works well in one situation, assumes that it is the ultimate answer to analyzing all performance, and begins applying it in a variety of nonfunctional ways, rather than examining the job environment with a variety of techniques to help the worker do the job more efficiently and effectively.

These limited-technique analysts are much like a carpenter with one tool—the hammer. Using a hammer in place of a saw or a level will certainly result in poor construction. So also, using one single analysis technique in all situations leads to little performance improvement. This is easily seen in organizations that view training as the ultimate solution to all performance problems. If problems exist, the analysis always results in using a trainer to talk about the problem. The organization might get sophisticated and bring in a microcomputer or multimedia presentation to tell employees how to perform, but the results are the same—usually poor. Employees return to the same work environment with increased knowledge, but without the ability or incentive to change the problem. The training, being costly and time-consuming, becomes part of the organization's problem, rather than a problem solution.

A single-solution analysis (training) often fails, just as a single-tool carpenter (hammer) builds poor houses. A set of analysis tools with a variety of well defined uses and a good structure or tool box in which to organize them are needed by those concerned with human performance improvement. That is the intent of this book, to describe a wide variety of analysis techniques, to suggest their most appropriate use, and to provide a structure for organizing them to improve human performance.

What Is the Structure of Analysis?

Analysis is a process which examines the component parts of some whole. The process of analyzing jobs and tasks involves at least three steps. First, the job or task is broken down into its component parts. Second, the relationships between the parts are examined and compared with correct principles of performance. Third, the parts are restructured to form an improved job or task, and learning requirements are specified.

The analyst breaks down the task by finding what the job is and then detailing how the job is done. The work *process* is described. Finding what the job is involves analysis techniques like the Interview Note Technique or the Card-Sort Technique which are described along with other closely related techniques in Chapter Two of this book. Detailing how the job is done requires analysis techniques like the Basic Task Description Technique or the Stimulus-Response Chart Technique described in Chapter Three.

The second step in the analysis process, which follows breaking down the task to find what it is and how it is done, is examining relationships between the parts of the task and the principles of correct performance. This details the *results* of the work. Chapter Four in this book describes various techniques used to examine the relationship between tasks and to correct performance and determine how to improve the job. These techniques include the

Critical Incident Technique and the Problem Analysis Technique, among others.

The third and final step in the analysis process is restructuring the job or task matching the principles of correct performance. This third step describes how the employee will learn the job and often involves a detailed training plan. Analysis techniques·used during this final step, which are described in Chapter 5, include the Master Plan Technique, Learning Objective Technique, and other closely related techniques.

No single-analysis technique completely covers the analysis process to break the task down, examine relationships, and restructure for learning. One technique might emphasize task breakdown. A second technique might be most concerned with specifying principles of correct performance. Another technique might generate training in the absence of correct performance principles. A good, complete analysis must cover each of the process steps. Therefore, any analysis situation requires the use of more than one technique. This book offers a variety of techniques which allow the analyst to complete the analysis process.

One might think of the analysis process as a tool box (Figure 1.1) containing compartments labeled task breakdown (finding what the job is and how it is done), relationship examination (finding how to improve the job), and task restructuring (finding how to learn the job). The tools in this box are the analysis techniques which will be discussed in this book. They fit in the various compartments of the analysis process according to their use. To analyze a job or task, the analyst uses the contents of the tool box to structure the analysis so that a correct fix is ensured.

What if the Analysis Is Incomplete?

Lengthy books containing job and task analyses that have *not* been used to change or improve the actual workplace can be found in some industries. One reason for this lack of use is that these analyses are incomplete. Some of the steps in the analysis process are missing. A long listing of detailed tasks may not define how the tasks should be structured for correct learning. An analysis

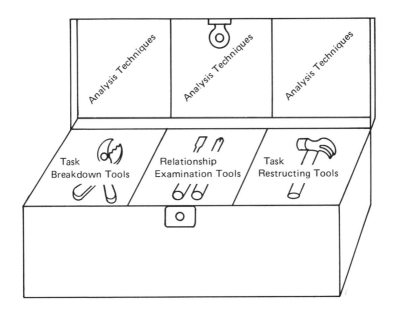

Figure 1.1. Analysis Tool Box.

based on correct principles of performance may not sufficiently detail the task components for employees to learn the task. Or perhaps a well-designed training course fails to meet a particular need and is left unused. If the analysis process does not proceed from task breakdown, through relationship analysis, to task restructuring, the results often go unused.

What General Skills Are Required?

Some basic skills are required of analysts who wish to improve job performance. Analysts must be skilled *observers, interviewers, questionnaire developers*, and *document collectors and analyzers*. As shown in Figure 1.2, these general skills are used throughout the techniques discussed in the various chapters of this book.

ANALYSIS SKILLS

PURPOSE	ANALYSIS TECHNIQUES	Interview	Group Work	Observation	Questionnaire	Document
Finding What The Job Is	Interview Note Technique	X	X			
	Card-Sort Technique	X	X		X	X
	Task Matrix Technique	X	X		X	X
	List Expansion Technique	X	X		X	X
	Daily Log Technique				X	X
	Walk and Talk Technique	X		X		
	Job Function Technique	X	X			
	Risk Assessment Technique				X	
Finding How the Job Is Done	Basic Task Description Technique	X	X	X	X	
	Stimulus-Response Chart Technique	X	X	X		
	Process Chart Technique			X		
	Operation Chart Technique	X		X		
	Man-Machine Time Chart Technique			X		
	Flow Chart Technique	X	X	X		
	Picture Technique	X	X	X		
	Decision Technique	X	X	X		
Finding How to Improve The Job	Basic Comparison Technique			X	X	
	Behavior Counting Technique	X	X	X		
	Path Analysis Technique	X		X	X	X
	Critical Incident Technique		X			
	Problem Analysis Technique	X	X	X		
	Performance Probe Technique	X	X	X		X
	Job Satisfaction Technique	X		X		
	Matrix Technique	X	X			
	Fault Tree Technique	X	X			
	Imagination Technique	X	X			
Finding How To Learn The Job	Master Plan Technique	X	X			X
	GUIDED Training Aid Technique	X	X	X		X
	Learning Objective Technique	X	X			X
	Learning Strategy Technique	X	X			X
	Learning Hierarchy Technique	X	X			X
	Pattern Note Technique	X	X			X

Figure 1.2. Analysis Techniques and Skills.

Observing. Observation is a skill used with many of the techniques described in this book. Analysts observe and record what workers actually do on the job rather than placing total reliance on what workers *say* they do. It helps identify elements of the job that are omitted from descriptions obtained with other methods. Observation makes any analysis more complete, reliable, and valid.

Some analysts claim that observation is the only valid method for analyzing jobs. This is incorrect. Observation should never be the only method used to analyze jobs. It has too many limitations. For instance, it is probably the most time-consuming technique. It is usually not feasible to observe enough people for long enough to analyze *all* tasks. In addition, observation is almost useless for analyzing jobs that consist of mostly mental tasks or very long and complex jobs. It works best for manual tasks which last only an hour or two.

The presence of the analyst causes further difficulties with observation. Workers usually perform differently when they are being watched until a "comfort level" is reached. If the observer uses a videotape recorder to "film" the worker, performance may be disrupted even more. The observer may record worker behaviors that have nothing to do with good performance, but result from the observation process itself.

One final concern with observation is the skill of the analysts. Inexperienced observers fail to note important things that workers do. Even experienced analysts tend to look at work in different ways. Some may note minute details while others record less detailed segments of behavior. Before observation is used, therefore, it is important to determine the level of behavior that is desired and to train the observers until they can all consistently record the desired behaviors in the same way.

If the technique selected to analyze the job includes observation, the analyst should use the following guidelines to ensure that the analysis is reliable and valid:

- Select observation only if the job is mostly manual and is not too complex or lengthy.
- Consider using observation to verify job data collected using other methods of analysis.

- Limit the analyst's impact on workers by reducing interference with the workers' activities. Only use video equipment if it is necessary to record very detailed actions. Stay in the workers' environment long enough to be accepted as part of the environment before analyzing the job. Consider actually becoming a participant or worker while analyzing the job.
- Train all observers to ensure that the same level of behavior is being recorded. Observers should do trial observations and meet after each trial to review their notes to ensure consistency. Actual analysis should not begin until observers demonstrate a pattern of consistency in their observation notes. Careful selection from the techniques suggested in this book should help reduce inconsistency.

Interviewing and Group Work. Interviews are necessary throughout the job analysis process. During interviews the analyst asks a worker or group of workers to describe the job. Interviews have definite advantages over observation. The worker becomes directly involved in the analysis process. This reduces the disruptive effects of formal observation. More information can be obtained with interviews than with any other technique. Time-consuming tasks are more easily recorded, and mental tasks and associated feelings are discovered. Information collected using other techniques can be clarified and expanded. Groups of workers can discuss and describe different work methods. Finally, the analysis can be flexible, permitting on-the-spot adaptation as needed instead of continuing an observation after it has become unfruitful.

Of course, interviews also have disadvantages for collecting information about jobs and tasks. The most serious is the subjectivity of the information collected. Each worker may have a different perspective about how the job should be done. The workers' descriptions may be incomplete or describe idealized work which is not actually done. The workers may not even be able to describe the job.

These disadvantages are somewhat alleviated by interviewing a group of experts together. A jury of experts can work as a group to iron out differences in perspective and to fill gaps in work descriptions. However, this approach also has difficulties, since the resulting job description may not reflect how any single worker does the job. For this reason, it is often best to follow up the group interview with actual observation of the job being performed.

A final difficulty with interviews concerns the analyst's technical skills. Planning skill is required to ensure that correct questions are being asked. Usually the questions must receive several trials before they match the analysis situation. Of course, the analyst's interpersonal skills reflect how well the questioning will be received by the workers. If the analyst cannot relate well to the workers, the data will be suspect. Time must be allowed for the workers to get to know the analyst. The time and skills required for planning, trials, and interpersonal association, combined with the difficulty of quantifying and summarizing the interview information, can make interviewing a difficult, time-consuming method.

The problems associated with interviewing can be overcome. The following considerations can be used to improve interviewing:

- Let interviews last no longer than one hour.
- Use tape recorders sparingly, since they bother some workers and increase data analysis time.
- Hold interviews in areas free from distractions.
- Consider workers' background, values, language, etc., when planning questions.
- Let workers think by allowing silence.
- Explain what you already know about the topic to save time.
- Pay attention to answers, not writing on forms.
- Engage in active listening (e.g., repeating answer or giving examples) to understand the worker.
- Observe expressions, actions, reactions, and related body talk.
- Start with broad questions before asking specifics.
- Conclude with informal conversation and a summary.

Questionnaires. Workers provide written answers to specific questions on questionnaires. This method has some obvious advantages. Information can be collected from many workers in a short period of time. The questionnaire can yield a great amount of information. Usually, the information can be summarized and reported easily. For these reasons, using questionnaires is a very cost-effective method for job analysis. Also, since the workers can spend time pondering the questions and because their responses can be anonymous, the collected information can be candid and reliable.

Questionnaires, however, are subject to several difficulties. Sometimes it is difficult to get a good rate of return, particularly with mailed questionnaires. This is a problem, since those who do return the questionnaires often have shared interests which could bias the results. A clearly written questionnaire that is understood by all of the workers is very difficult to construct, and confusion and ambiguity cannot be clarified by an interviewer until the questionnaire is returned. Usually, there is limited provision for free expression, so real problems and solutions may be overlooked. Finally, illiterate, semi-literate, and mixed-culture groups of workers will certainly provide erroneous and varying responses. When the selected analysis technique requires the use of questionnaires, the following considerations should be noted:

- *Determine the questionnaire's purpose.* It often helps to interview or observe workers before constructing the questionnaire. The number of topics should be identified and incorporated into the questionnaire. The distribution and required rate of return should be specified.
- *Design the questionnaire.* Write clearly, concisely, with short sentences, yet ensure that all needed information is solicited. Start with basic information; then get more specific. Order the questions logically. Use examples to explain difficult questions. Use close-ended responses whenever possible since they are easier to summarize, but include open-ended questions to allow for explanations. Avoid emotionally charged wording and leading questions.
- *Pretest and revise the questionnaire.* Other analysts might complete the questionnaire, or a few selected workers might complete it to ensure it is understandable and that it

is collecting all required information. The pretest checks the directions to the worker, the sequencing of the questions, and the questionnaire's overall appearance.

- *Distribute the questionnaire.* Determine who will receive the questionnaire—everyone for small audiences versus some random sample of workers for large audiences. The mailed questionnaire should include a cover letter and a self-addressed, stamped envelope.

Documents. The collection and analysis of job-related documents are essential skills for analysts. Important documents include job descriptions, resumes, management objective lists, training materials, work accounting records, job procedures, equipment descriptions, personnel records, job-related texts, and previously completed analyses of related jobs. These documents provide uncensored information about the job and expectations concerning it. Using such documents often greatly reduces the need for initial observation and interviewing, thus making the analysis much less costly.

Of course, all needed information may not be documented, or the analyst may not be given access to sensitive documents. This reduces the number of useful documents; but the analyst should always begin an analysis by inquiring into the availability of job-related documents.

Conducting the Analysis

Every analysis, despite the techniques selected, uses the following general steps and considerations to ensure that an appropriate solution is reached in an orderly fashion:

1. Complete an analysis agreement as discussed in the following section. The analysis agreement should specify the purpose of the analysis, including what the job is, how the job is done, how the job could be improved, and how the job should be learned. The analysis agreement also specifies how the workers' background, environment, attitudes, and knowledge will influence the analysis. Finally, the analysis agreement should specify the analysis techniques to be used. A variety of techniques can be used, depending upon the situation, to analyze a job. Each

technique provides unique advantages and disadvantages, summarized in the other chapters in this book. The basic skills of observing, interviewing and group work, constructing questionnaires, and analyzing documents are required throughout the techniques.

2. Conduct trials using the analysis techniques to train analysts and to anticipate problems. If needed, revisions can be made before the official analysis begins.

3. Schedule analysis sessions well in advance to allow time for participants to prepare. If possible, schedule the analysis through the immediate supervisor to assure the master performer that it is important and approved. Avoid scheduling analysis sessions late in the day, just before weekends, or just after lunch. Try to arrange for a pleasant, quiet setting without distractions or observers. Send out a follow-up memo of the schedule.

4. Conduct the analysis as planned using the selected techniques. These techniques should break down the task, examine important relationships, and restructure the task. (The actual steps used by each technique are discussed in the chapters which follow.) Do not be afraid to change techniques if analysis shows that another direction would be more helpful. Use of a technique often modifies the course of the analysis; however, these changes must be communicated to the participants by renegotiating the analysis agreement.

5. Organize and analyze the data immediately after it is collected to clarify meaning, solve problem areas, and plan for additional analysis. This helps ensure that nothing is overlooked and greatly increases the timeliness of analysis completion. It is necessary to plan for this data review activity and allot time for it in the analysis schedule.

6. Follow up each data collection session with a formal memo reviewing the results and thanking the participants. This helps maintain cordial relations and prepares the participants for any future analysis sessions.

7. Complete a detailed report summarizing the entire analysis. (This report is discussed in the last chapter of this book.)

Arranging an Analysis Agreement

The first step in analyzing a job is to define precisely what will be done. Most individuals who desire a job analysis do not fully understand what is required or what is possible. Yet, they frequently have some idea of a final product. For instance, they might say they want to create training, write job descriptions, or solve performance problems. They usually want to leave the details of how the analysis is conducted to the expert—the analyst.

In one way, this is nice for the analyst, who as an expert need only apply those techniques with which he or she is familiar. However, problems often occur if the analyst's techniques turn out a result that does not meet the client's needs. When this occurs, the analysis results are seldom used, the analysis effort and resources are wasted, and the analyst is not asked back.

To ensure that the analyst and other parties agree on expected analysis results, it is important to create a clear, understandable, and precise description of the analysis. This analysis agreement is equally essential whether the analyst is an outside consultant or an in-house trainer.

The following material introduces the requirements of and methods for producing an effective analysis agreement. *The format of this material is the same as that of the remaining techniques in this book.*

The purpose of the technique is covered in a short sentence. This is followed by advantages and disadvantages of the technique, and the steps in the technique. Finally, an example is provided showing one practical application of the technique.

ANALYSIS AGREEMENT TECHNIQUE

Purpose

The Analysis Agreement Technique is used to establish an understanding between the analyst and client about the goals, responsibilities, methods, and results of the job analysis.

Advantages

The Analysis Agreement Technique ensures the successful completion of the project. It tends to reduce threats and misunderstandings common in job analysis situations. It makes time and resource commitments explicit. It clarifies goals, expectations, tasks, and results. It sets up a realistic management system and lets clients know how much effort will be required to achieve their goals. Finally, the agreement gives a framework for documenting the final analysis results and completing the final report.

Disadvantages

The Analysis Agreement Technique requires careful front-end planning. This may be frustrating to a supervisor who is concerned about getting the job improved *now*, or having training quickly available. This technique forces clients and analysts into a professional relationship that might seem too formal—especially for in-house trainers.

Description

The analyst meets with the perspective client and plans the Analysis Agreement. This process is flow-charted in Figure 1.3 and uses the following steps:

1. *Contact the client and assess the situation.* A good agreement cannot be made until the analyst understands the client's environment, the perceived problems, the proposed solutions, and other general information about the client's needs. With some clients this can be learned after a short meeting. Other situations may require several meetings and even some initial observation and interviewing before the agreement can be written.

2. *Introduce the analysis agreement technique.* This is done by defining the various sections of the agreement and sharing how the analysis typically proceeds. With some clients a tentative agreement can be established immediately after the introduction. Others require several additional meetings to work out the various sections of the agreement. In any case, the analyst should discuss the need for each of the following sections:

   - ○ **Overview** stating the general intent of the analysis.
   - ○ **Personnel** who will be involved including supervisors, analyst, and master performers.
   - ○ **Main Goals** stating what the analysis will generally accomplish.
   - ○ **Objectives** stating specifically what will be done.
   - ○ **Methods** and techniques which will be used to meet the objectives.
   - ○ **Resources** which will be needed to complete the analysis.
   - ○ **Management** stating how the analysis will be supervised to ensure it proceeds without problems.
   - ○ **Products** and other results which will be provided at the completion of the analysis.
   - ○ **Evaluation** stating how analysis adequacy will be judged.

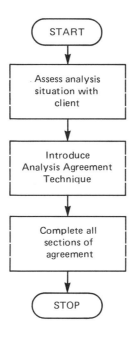

Figure 1.3. Analysis Agreement Technique.

- ○ **Renegotiation** stating how changes in the analysis will be accommodated.
- ○ **Signatures** space for the analyst and client to sign and date the agreement.

3. Complete each section of the agreement. The client and analyst discuss what is needed to do the analysis and write their decisions. It is usually best to start with the goals of the analysis, to specify objectives, and to list the methods to be used. This leads into the other sections of the agreement. The finished agreement should be typed, signed, and dated. The agreement should then be used throughout the analysis as a guide and communication tool.

Example

An analyst was asked to examine the job of room attendants (sometimes called maids) at a large hotel. The analyst met with the hotel manager to assess the environment, perceived problems, proposed solutions, and related information. The manager indicated that he wanted to improve the room attendants' performance. After a period of discussion, the analyst introduced the idea of an analysis agreement. This lead to discussion of the various sections of the agreement. The analyst returned to his office and jotted down some ideas in the form of a tentative agreement. The next day the analyst and hotel manager met to review the tentative ideas and produce a formal agreement. The agreement which resulted is shown in Figure 1.4.

Chapter Summary

A good, usable analysis of jobs and tasks breaks down the performance into its component parts to find the process used, then examines important relationships between the process and correct performance to assess effective results, and finally restructures the process so it can be learned and performed. This three-part analysis process structures the selection of correct analysis techniques for each job situation.

Many techniques can be used. The use of a single favorite technique for every situation results in weak, inappropriate, partial, and unused analyses. To counter this the analyst *must select several techniques* to complete all steps in the analysis process. This book gives guidance for selecting these techniques.

The analyst begins the analysis with an agreement specifying what will be done. This improves communication and helps ensure proper results. Skill in observing, interviewing, using questionnaires, and analyzing documents is required throughout the analysis. With these skills and a specific agreement, the analyst only needs to follow the steps in the selected techniques to complete a valid and useful analysis of the job.

The chapters which follow introduce the various techniques needed to complete an analysis correctly. Chapter Two discusses finding what the job is. Chapter Three is about finding how the job should be done. Chapter Five shows the determination of how to learn the job. Finally, Chapter Six discusses completion of the analysis and the final report.

OVERVIEW
This agreement describes the proposed analysis of the room attendant job at the ABC Hotel.

PERSONNEL
Hotel Manager—Bill Randolph
Analyst—Ken Carlisle
Housekeeping Supervisor—Ronda Wells
Master Performers—Juanita Lopez, Sharon Anderson, Chi Ling

GOAL
To improve room attendants' performance by analyzing the job and determining training requirements.

OBJECTIVES
1. To list the specific tasks done by the room attendant.
2. To detail critical tasks and provide job aids.
3. To determine supervisory requirements.
4. To specify learning objectives for skills needing training.

METHODS
1. The Interview Note Technique, Card-Sort Technique, and Walk and Talk Technique will be used to list the specific tasks done by room attendants.
2. The Risk Assessment Technique will be used to determine task criticality.
3. The Flow Chart Technique, Decision Technique, and Picture Technique will be used to detail how the critical tasks are done.
4. The Performance Probe Technique will be used to determine supervisory and information requirements for the room attendants.
5. The Master Plan Technique, GUIDED Training Aid Technique, and Learning Objective Technique will be used to summarize the training and other requirements needed for correct performance.

RESOURCES
1. Time must be allowed to interview and observe master performers.
2. Position description and content related materials must be made available.
3. Travel to several hotels will be required.

MANAGEMENT
The hotel manager will review the analysis results. The housekeeping supervisor will interface directly with the analyst to schedule interviews and observations. The analyst will be responsible for completing the analysis on schedule.

PRODUCTS
The final report will include a task inventory, job aids for critical tasks, supervisory checksheets, training objectives, and a master planning guide for use in implementing the analysis results.

EVALUATION
The housekeeping supervisor will evaluate the content of the various resulting products. The hotel manager will assess the adequacy of the analysis in meeting this agreement.

Figure 1.4. Example Analysis Agreement

RENEGOTIATION
Any portion of this agreement may be revised at any time by mutual consent of the personnel involved.

SIGNATURES

....
Hotel Manager

....
Date

....
Housekeeping Supervisor

....
Date

....
Analyst

....
Date

Figure 1.4 (Continued)

2

Finding What the Job Is

"What is the job?" This is usually the first question asked when analyzing a job. In answer, the position title is usually stated— baker, mechanic, secretary, instructor, supervisor, accountant, banker, etc. This is a good starting point, but the job title by itself fails to clearly *define* the job. A baker not only bakes, but also heats, kneads, measures, rolls, seasons, spreads, mixes, etc., while using various tools, materials, and types of equipment. A good job description lists the job title, the actions performed, and the objects used.

Main Goal: To Write Task Statements

Jobs are described with short sentences containing the actions performed and the objects involved in the performance. These sentences are called *task statements*. Each task statement describes a goal-directed activity or group of activities. If many activities are grouped under the task statement, it is called a duty. If a task statement describes a single activity, it is called a task. A task statement might only describe a portion of a single activity. This is usually called a task element. These distinctions are shown in Figure 2.1. Jobs consist of "duties" with many activities, which are made of single "tasks," which consist of "task elements."

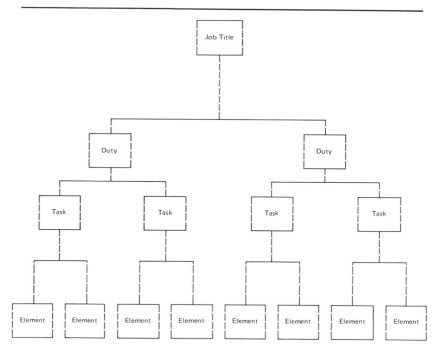

Figure 2.1. Task Statement Levels.

The distinction between duties, tasks, and task elements, however, is not really important to the process of writing task statements. The duties of some jobs are tasks for other jobs, and task elements may be the important tasks of very detailed specific jobs. In practice, any task statement may be made more general or divided into finer detail. However, in all cases the task statements are written in the same way. Task statements all have actions and objects. The following list shows good task statements:

Actions	Objects
Disassemble	Valves
Clean	Rugs
Operate	Forklifts
Determine	Load Limits
Supervise	Projects

POOR TASK STATEMENT	RULE	GOOD TASK STATEMENT
Consolidate and separate important documentation	Use easily understood wording	File documents
Have responsibility for instructors	Use precise action verbs	Supervise instructors
Prepare forms that tell mechanics to perform various jobs	Be brief	Fill out work orders
Operate and maintain vacuum gages	Avoid "and" which implies two tasks	1—Operate vacuum gages 2—Maintain vacuum gages
Calculate NPSH	Use complete statements, avoid abbreviations	Calculate Net Positive Suction Head
Enjoy operating the word processor	Do not include attitudes	Operate the word processor
Use math skills to calculate load limits	Do not include knowledge or experience requirements	Calculate load limits
Learn correct document filing procedures	Do not include required training	File documents
You repair magnetic drives	The subject "I" or "you" is understood	Repair magnetic drives

Figure 2.2. Task Statements.

Task statements must be clear, specific, precise, complete yet brief, and relevant to the activity being defined. Rules for writing task statements, along with good examples and poor examples, are shown in Figure 2.2.

A clearly communicated definition of the job results from a completed listing of task statements. The completed list is called a task inventory. The rest of this chapter describes various techniques for developing a task inventory. Each technique has unique purposes, advantages, and disadvantages.

INTERVIEW NOTE TECHNIQUE

Purpose
The Interview Note Technique is used to record and detail task statements elicited during interviews with master performers.

Advantages
The Interview Note Technique requires no special forms—a regular note pad is adequate. The analyst does not need to have any initial understanding of the job before the interview. It is a very appropriate technique for detailing task statements.

Disadvantages
The Interview Note Technique is time-consuming and therefore costly. Since the analyst usually records the notes, the master performer cannot easily see an overall picture of the analysis as the interview progresses. As a result, it is difficult to ensure that all task statements are identified with this technique.

Description
The analyst interviews a master performer to determine and detail task statements. This process is flow-charted in Figure 2.3 and uses the following steps:
1. List job title at the top of the note page.
2. Divide the note page into three columns as illustrated in Figure 2.4.
3. Ask the following question: "What are the main duties of this job?"
4. List each main duty with a consecutive number.
5. After all main duties are listed, draw a horizontal line across the page to separate the list of main duties from the first detailing list.

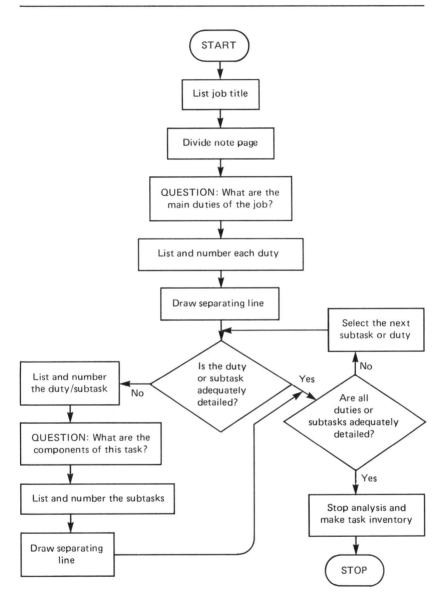

Figure 2.3. Interview Note Technique.

6. Determine if each main duty needs to be detailed. If not, list the reason for stopping analysis in the right column and select the next main duty. If a duty needs detailing, continue with the method. The following rules are used to determine how much to detail task statements.

   Rule 1—*Continue adding detail until adequate to meet the situation's objectives.* For instance, if a subject matter expert will use the analysis to develop training materials, little detail is required.

   Rule 2—*Continue adding detail until the analysis overlaps other analysis questions.* For instance, stop writing task statements when the master performer begins describing "how" the task is done rather than "what" the task is.

   Rule 3—*Continue adding detail until an intermediate level is reached.* For instance, "repair engines" may be too general and "remove carburetor bolts" may be too detailed. The correct level might be to "repair carburetors."

   Rule 4—*Continue adding detail to very difficult and critical tasks.* If performance error is likely and if the error is associated with high costs because of personnel injury, equipment repair, material usage, or public reaction, then the task statements should be very detailed. Easily understood and accomplished tasks do not need additional detailing (see the Risk Assessment Technique in this chapter).

   Rule 5—*Err in the direction of too little detail* unless it is very expensive to reanalyze the task. It will quickly become evident if there is too little detail to improve the job or to develop training and the analysis can be continued. However, if it is too detailed, the costs of gaining the extra detail will have been wasted.

7. Write the main duty or subtask and its number. Then ask the following question to identify more detailed subtasks: "What are the components of this task?"

8. List the subtasks of the duty, task, or subtask using the following numbering system:

                    1.0
                      1.1
                      1.2
                      Etc.
                            1.1.1
                            1.1.2
                            Etc.
                                  1.1.1.1
                                  1.1.1.2
                                  Etc.
                    2.0
                    Etc.

9. After all the subtasks of a main duty are listed, draw a horizontal line across the page to separate the next section.
10. Apply the depth-of-analysis rules in step 6 to determine if each subtask needs to be detailed. If not, list the reason for stopping analysis in the right column and select the next subtask. If the subtask needs detailing, return to Step 7 and continue detailing until all subtasks are identified.
11. Stop analysis when all duties, tasks, subtasks, sub-subtasks, etc., are adequately detailed.
12. Reorganize the interview notes into a completed task inventory.

Example

The secretary position at a small consulting firm was analyzed using the interview note technique. Figure 2.4 shows the notes that were taken while

NUMBER	TASK STATEMENT	REASON ANALYSIS STOPPED

1.
2.
3.
4.
5.
	File documents
	Greet visitors
	Answer telephone
	Maintain office supplies
	Type letters
		1. Continue analysis
		2., 3. Stop analysis since
		          tasks are very easy
		4. Continue analysis
		5. Stop analysis since
		          secretary is expert
		          typist

1.
1.1
1.2
1.3
1.4
1.5
	File documents
	Determine document topic
	Fill out subject card(s)
	Assign document number
	Place document in file drawer
	Place subject card(s) in card file
		1.1 Continue analysis
		1.2 to 1.5 Stop analysis,
		          secretary will learn
		          these tasks by being
		          shown one time

1.1
1.1.1
1.1.2
1.1.3
	Determine document topic
	Read document title
	Read document introduction
	Read document summary
		1.1.1 to 1.1.3 Stop
		          analysis since fur-
		          ther analysis con-
		          cerns how to read

4.
4.1
 	
4.2
	Maintain office supplies
	Complete required materials
	   checklist
	Order supplies
		4.1 Stop, checklist
		          easily understood
		4.2 Stop, easy checklist

Figure 2.4. Example Interview Note Technique.

interviewing a secretary. Five duties were identified; only duties one (File Documents) and four (Maintain Office Supplies) were detailed. Duty one (File Documents) was found to involve five subtasks, one of which required further detailing (1.1).

After the notes were taken, they were rewritten as task statements to form the following task inventory:

    1.0 File documents
          1.1 Determine document type
               1.1.1 Read document title
               1.1.2 Read document introduction
               1.1.3 Read document summary
          1.2 Fill out subject card(s)
          1.3 Assign document number
          1.4 Place document in file drawer
          1.5 Place subject card(s) in card file
    2.0 Greet visitors
    3.0 Answer telephone
    4.0 Maintain office supplies
          4.1 Complete required materials checklist
          4.2 Order necessary supplies
    5.0 Type letters

CARD-SORT TECHNIQUE

Purpose

The Card-Sort Technique is used to record task statements found while reviewing documents which describe what personnel do.

Advantages

The Card-Sort Technique lets the analyst immediately record any task statement encountered, without requiring an understanding of the relationship of the task to any other task. Therefore, documents require only one review. After all documents are reviewed, the task statement cards can be easily reordered. The task statements are usually identified without the help of a master performer, so interview and observation time as well as associated costs are reduced.

Disadvantages

The reordering of many task statement cards can be time-consuming and may require the help of a master performer if the job is very complex.

Interviews with master performers are required after typing task inventories to ensure that task statements are correct and complete.

Description

The analyst reviews documents which describe the job to identify task statements. This process is flow-charted in Figure 2.5 and uses the following steps:

1. Collect task statement source documents from the workplace. Example source documents include job descriptions, resumes, management objective lists, training materials, job procedures, equipment descriptions, job-related texts, and task inventories of related jobs. It is quite possible that task inventories for similar jobs already exist that can be used with little or no modification. Since this eliminates the need for detailed analysis, it is a very cost-effective alternative.
2. Review each source document. Whenever a task statement is identified, write it on a separate 3 x 5 card. Do not indicate relationship order on the card unless it is clearly indicated in the source document.
3. Sort the cards into a logical, sequential order after all documents are reviewed. Some cards may have to be rewritten to maintain consistent wording of related tasks. If the job is very complex, a master performer may have to complete the card sort.
4. Number the reordered tasks sequentially. Task groupings may be indicated with scientific notation, 1.0, 1.1, 1.2, 1.2.1, 2.0, etc.
5. Type the task statements into an initial task inventory using one of the formats discussed in this chapter.
6. Have a master performer review the task inventory to ensure that the tasks are actually performed, correctly worded, and complete. The other techniques in this chapter may be used at this point to format and detail task statements.
7. Revise task statements to reflect the master performer's review, then produce the completed task inventory.

Example

Documents describing the job of Super Chicken's short order cook were reviewed and task statements written on separate 3 x 5 cards. A sample of these cards is shown in Figure 2.6. These cards were sorted, edited, sequentially numbered, reviewed by a master performer, and eventually typed as the following task inventory:

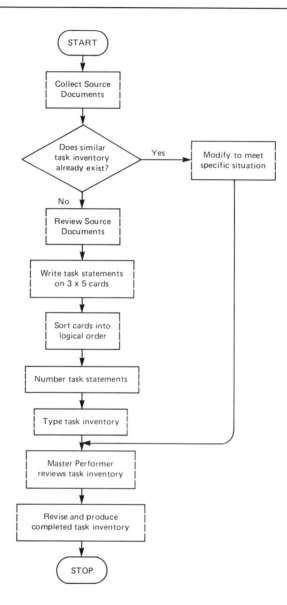

Figure 2.5. Card-Sort Technique.

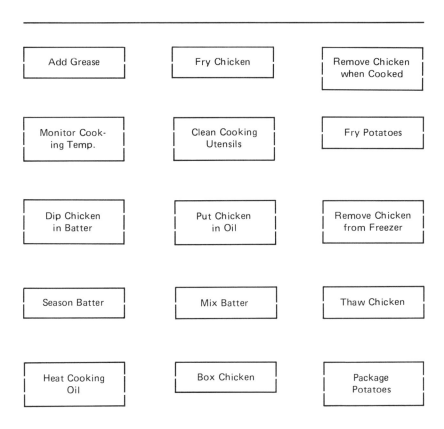

Figure 2.6. Example Task Statement Cards.

1.0 Prepare fry cooker
    1.1 Add cooking oil
    1.2 Heat cooking oil
    1.3 Monitor cooking oil temperature
2.0 Cook fried chicken
    2.1 Remove chicken from freezer
    2.2 Thaw chicken
    2.3 Season batter
    2.4 Mix batter
    2.5 Dip chicken in batter

       2.6 Put chicken in cooking oil

       2.7 Monitor chicken until cooked

       2.8 Remove chicken when cooked

   3.0 Cook fried potatoes

       3.1 Remove fried potatoes from freezer

       3.2 Pour fried potatoes in cooking oil

       3.3 Monitor fried potatoes until cooked

       3.4 Remove fried potatoes when cooked

   4.0 Package Super Chicken meal

       4.1 Box fried chicken

       4.2 Package fried potatoes

       4.3 Put fried potatoes in fried chicken box

       4.4 Put packaged meal on service counter

   5.0 Clean cooking area

       5.1 Clean fry cooker

       5.2 Clean cooking utensils

       5.3 Empty garbage cans

       5.4 Mop floors

TASK MATRIX TECHNIQUE

Purpose

The Task Matrix Technique is used to arrange the actions performed and objects acted upon so that master performers can easily identify task statements. It works best when the job consists of a few basic actions performed with various people or types of equipment.

Advantages

The Task Matrix Technique can greatly reduce interview or questionnaire development and completion time because task statements are abbreviated for easy review. Bulky task inventories can be greatly reduced in size. This technique also ensures a standardized consideration of each task from a broad perspective.

Disadvantages

A detailed job-related document review or interview is necessary before a good task matrix can be developed. This method is difficult to use when a job consists of a large variety of different actions because the matrix becomes too large and cumbersome. It is therefore less useful for detailing tasks.

Description

The analyst formats task statements into a comprehensive matrix. This process is flow-charted in Figure 2.7 and uses the following steps:

1. Either review job-related documents and identify all actions performed and objects acted upon (the Card Sort Technique might be used), or interview a master performer using the Interview Note Technique.
2. Categorize all identified actions to eliminate redundancy and list them across the top of a matrix sheet (see Figures 2.8 and 2.13). There will usually be fewer actions than objects to be acted upon.
3. List all objects associated with the actions down the side of the matrix. The listed objects will vary greatly with the type of job. Management jobs tend to include people, paper, materials, and office supplies, whereas operator jobs tend to include long lists of equipment, or systems like those shown in Figure 2.8 (in this instance, for a water treatment facility operator).
4. Review the completed matrix with a master performer after the initial draft is created. The master performer should add any important actions and objects which were missed. If the action does not apply to a listed object, it should be left blank. All matrix matches which apply to the job should be checked. When most actions apply to most objects, it is easier to reverse the checking process and only check (or "X" out) those action/object matches which do *not* apply to the job (see Figure 2.8).
5. Rewrite the action/object pairs as a formal task inventory.

Example

The following is a small excerpt from the position description of a water treatment facility operator. It was reviewed and important actions and objects were underlined.

> "The water treatment facility operator operates all plant systems, and is responsible to adjust systems and repair problem equipment so as to ensure high quality water reclamation."

The actions and objects of this passage, along with the actions and objects found in other documents, were categorized and listed on the matrix shown in Figure 2.8. A master performer "X'd" out those matrix matches which *did not* apply to the water treatment operator's job. Then the following task statements were written:

    1.0 Trickling Filters

        1.1 Locate the trickling filters

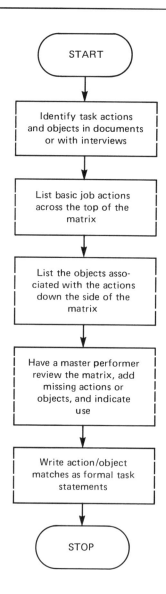

Figure 2.7. Task Matrix Technique.

| JOB: WATER TREATMENT OPERATOR | | | | |
EQUIPMENT/ACTIONS	LOCATE	OPERATE	ADJUST	REPAIR
1. Trickling Filters				X
2. First-Stage Clarifiers				X
3. Lime Slaking, Feeding, and Transfer System				X
4. Polymer System				
5. Domestic Water System				
6. Process Water System				

Figure 2.8. Water Treatment Operator Task Matrix.

    1.2 Operate the trickling filters
    1.3 Adjust trickling filter flow
2.0 First Stage Clarifiers
    2.1 Locate the first-stage clarifiers
    2.2 Operate the first-stage clarifiers
    2.3 Adjust first-rate clarifiers' flow
3.0 Lime Slaking, Feeding, and Transfer System
    3.1 Locate the lime slaking, feeding, and transfer system
    3.2 Operate the lime slaking, feeding, and transfer system
    3.3 Adjust the lime slaking, feeding, and transfer system
4.0 Polymer System
    4.1 Locate the polymer system
    4.2 Operate the polymer system
    4.3 Adjust the polymer system
5.0 Domestic Water System
    5.1 Locate the domestic water system
    5.2 Operate the domestic water system
    5.3 Adjust the domestic water system
    5.4 Repair the domestic water system
6.0 Process Water System
    6.1 Locate the process water system
    6.2 Operate the process water system
    6.3 Adjust the process water system
    6.4 Repair the process water system

LIST EXPANSION TECHNIQUE

Purpose

The List Expansion Technique is another technique used to structure interview or questionnaire data. It works well when the job requires many actions using numerous tools or types of equipment.

Advantages

The List Expansion Technique reduces task statements to a simplified and categorized list which can be reviewed and detailed easily. Its main advantage over the Task Matrix Technique is the ease with which additional objects and actions in each category can be added and detailed. The listing format also produces completed task statements.

Disadvantages

Detailed job-related documents or interviews must be available for review—a necessary first step with this technique. The task receives less standardized consideration with this technique than with the Task Matrix Technique so it works best when analyzing jobs that consist of a large variety of objects and actions which do not necessarily have standardized functions, i.e., do not all involve a common action like weld, screw, or type.

Description

The analyst formats task statements into a comprehensive list. This process is flow-charted in Figure 2.9 and uses the following steps:

1. Review job-related documents and underline all actions performed and objects acted upon.
2. Categorize all objects, types of equipment, materials, etc., and list them. The Card Sort Technique is helpful during this step.
3. Detail all actions which are used and list them under the appropriate object.
4. Have a master performer review the list and expand it as needed by adding actions or objects in response to the following two questions: "What are the types of related equipment, materials, etc.?" and "What other actions are performed?"
5. Rewrite the actions and objects as formal task statements if needed. Often, this is not necessary because the listing format tends to produce task statements.

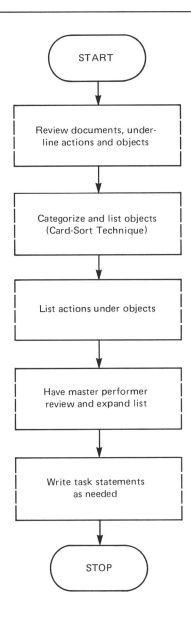

Figure 2.9. List Expansion Technique.

Example

A power plant equipment operator's job description was reviewed and important actions and objects were underlined. The following excerpt shows this process:

"The power plant equipment operator operates lifting and transferring equipment like cranes, fork lifts, cars, and trucks, and associated equipment like rigging."

The job analyst's initial review of this job-related document produced the following partial list:

    1.0 Operate Cranes
        1.1 Raise load
        1.2 Lower load
        1.3 Transfer load
    2.0 Operate Forklifts
        2.1 Load
        2.2 Lift
        2.3 Transfer
    3.0 Rigging
        3.1 Sling equipment
        3.2 Prepare rigging
        3.3 Test load

During the final review the master performer added the types of equipment and actions shown in parentheses in the following list:

    1.0   Operate Cranes (Bridges, Mobile, Shop)
        1.1   Raise load
        1.2   Lower load
        1.3   Transfer load
        (1.4   Manipulate load)
        (1.5   Route load)
        (1.6   Blind lift load)
        (1.7   Determine load limit)
        (1.8   Inspect rigging)
        (1.9   Communicate with hand signals)
    2.0   Operate Forklifts (Electric, Diesel)
        2.1   Load
        2.2   Lift
        2.3   Transfer
        (2.4   Lower)
        (2.5   Unload)

3.0 Rigging (Slings, Scaffolding)
    3.1 Sling equipment
    3.2 Prepare rigging
    3.3 Test load
    (3.4 Evaluate rigging condition)

DAILY LOG TECHNIQUE

Purpose

The Daily Log Technique is used to determine task statements when job-related documents do not exist and the master performer is unable to state precisely how the job is performed.

Advantages

This technique reduces subjectivity by having the master performer record what is actually done, rather than what is *thought* to be done. It is very useful for analyzing supervisor or management positions, since these frequently contain activities that are easily forgotten or difficult to assess. This technique also details the amount of time spent on various activities.

Disadvantages

Data collection with this technique is costly in terms of master performer time. It may take weeks or even months before all activities are performed and the logs completed.

Description

The analyst helps the master performer log daily activities. This process is flow-charted in Figure 2.10 and uses the following steps:

1. Have a master performer keep a log of daily activities over a period of time (see Figure 2.11). The activity, time, and explanation should be recorded in the log. The log should be kept until all major tasks have been performed at least once.
2. Review the log and underline all actions performed and objects acted upon.
3. Categorize and list all activities and objects, and continue the analysis using either the Interview Note Technique, Card Sort Technique, Task Matrix Technique, or List Expansion Technique.

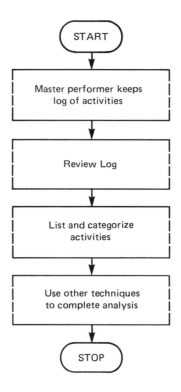

Figure 2.10. Daily Log Technique.

Example

A training manager was asked to keep a daily log. Figure 2.11 shows a half-day of the log which was reviewed by the analyst. Important actions and objects were underlined. The following list of task statements was then written:

1. Solicit information
2. Talk on telephone
3. Talk to individuals
4. Read mail
5. Review documents

JOB: TRAINING MANAGER		DATE: 9/24/84
TIME	ACTIVITY	EXPLANATION
8:00 - 8:30	Solicited and submitted daily time cards.	I called to remind two employees to complete their time cards. I reviewed each time card to ensure it was correct, recorded overtime and absence in the record book, and sent the cards to payroll.
	Answered telephone call.	Vendor called to discuss possible services. I asked that information on his services be sent.
8:30 - 9:00	Read mail from previous day	Wrote short messages on some of the mail encouraging different types of action and routed it to various individuals. Placed several vendor service descriptions in the "to be filed" drawer. Discarded several others.
9:00 - 10:30	Met with personnel manager	Discussed various alternatives for getting staff to develop a required training program. Decided on three alternatives.
10:30- 11:00	Met with training analyst	Discussed a needs assessment that was being done and suggested several ways that it might proceed.
11:00- 12:00	Wrote a justification for contracting a vendor to evaluate the training function.	The writing involved the review of several related documents and one phone call to the bid processor.

Figure 2.11. Daily Log for Training Manager.

6. Discuss alternative actions
7. Decide alternatives
8. Instruct individuals to act
9. Submit time cards
10. Write justifications
11. Write messages

WALK AND TALK TECHNIQUE

Purpose

The Walk and Talk Technique is used to remind the master performer of the types of equipment, materials, and activities used when doing a job so that task statements can be written.

Advantages

This technique results in a very precise and complete listing of the equipment, materials, or activities used to perform the task by reminding the master performer of what is actually done.

Disadvantages

This technique can be time-consuming. For example, going through a mechanic's tool box could take days.

Description

The analyst tours the workplace with the master performer to identify tools, equipment, materials, and activities. This process is flow-charted in Figure 2.12 and uses the following steps:

1. Tour the workplace with the master performer.
2. Have the master performer point out each piece of equipment or material that is being used and what the various workers are doing.
3. List the types of equipment, materials, and activities, and continue the analysis using the Interview Note Technique, Task Matrix Technique, or List Expansion Technique.

Example

While analyzing a water treatment facility chemist position, the analyst and a master chemist toured the lab. The master chemist pointed to various pieces of equipment and described briefly how each was used. The analyst listed the following equipment:

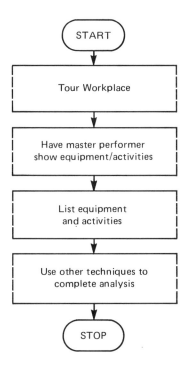

Figure 2.12. Walk and Talk Technique.

1. Viscometer
2. pH Meter
3. Automatic Titrator
4. Amperometric Titrator
5. Manual Titrator
6. Ion Electrodes
7. UV Visible Spectrophotometer
8. Centrifuge
9. Microscope
10. Autoclave
11. Digestion Apparatus

12. Turbidimeter
13. Distillation Apparatus
14. Hydrometer
15. Test Kits
16. Carbon Analyzer
17. Conductivity Meter
18. Balance

Based upon the above list, the analyst prepared the Task Matrix shown in Figure 2.13. The master chemist then checked all combinations which were

JOB: WATER TREATMENT CHEMIST				
EQUIPMENT/ACTIONS	LOCATE	OPERATE	CALI-BRATE	TROUBLE-SHOOT
1. Viscometer	✓	✓	✓	✓
2. pH Meter	✓	✓	✓	✓
3. Automatic Titrator	✓	✓	✓	✓
4. Amperometric Titrator	✓	✓	✓	✓
5. Manual Titrator	✓	✓	✓	
6. Ion Electrodes	✓	✓	✓	✓
7. UV Visible Spectrophotometer	✓	✓	✓	✓
8. Centrifuge	✓	✓	✓	✓
9. Microscope	✓	✓	✓	✓
10. Autoclave	✓	✓	✓	✓
11. Digestion Apparatus	✓	✓	✓	✓
12. Turbidimeter	✓	✓	✓	✓
13. Distillation Apparatus	✓	✓	✓	✓
14. Hydrometer	✓	✓	✓	
15. Test Kits	✓	✓	✓	
16. Carbon Analyzer	✓	✓	✓	✓
17. Conductivity Meter	✓	✓	✓	✓
18. Balance	✓	✓	✓	✓

Figure 2.13. Water Treatment Chemist Task Matrix.

part of the job. Task statements were then derived from the Task Matrix as shown in the following partial listing:

1.0 Viscometer

    1.1 Locate the viscometer

    1.2 Operate the viscometer

    1.3 Calibrate the viscometer

    1.4 Troubleshoot the viscometer

2.0 pH Meter

    2.1 Locate the pH meter

    2.2 Operate the pH meter

    2.3 Calibrate the pH meter

    2.4 Troubleshoot the pH meter

3.0 Etc.

JOB FUNCTION TECHNIQUE

Purpose

The Job Function Technique provides standardized categories which can be used to identify and organize specific tasks.

Advantages

The complete coverage of tasks is better ensured when inventories are compared against a master listing of standard job functions. Categorization also allows easy comparison of different jobs and tasks. The categories speed up the process of identifying task statements, and permit using standardized language.

Disadvantages

Job functions tend to reduce the amount of detail in task statements and also reduce the job-specific language of task statements. In some situations, especially highly technical areas, some job functions may be omitted.

Description

The analyst and master performer review possible job functions to determine task statements. This process is flow-charted in Figure 2.14 and uses the following steps:

1. Review each of the job functions shown in Figure 2.15 with the master performer.
2. Have the master performer identify all job functions that relate to the job.

3. Identify the specific actions performed and information, people, and things related to each job function. Then, write task statements.
4. Continue analysis as needed using one of the other techniques in this chapter to complete a task inventory.

Example

A plant equipment operator instructor was asked to analyze his job by reviewing the job functions shown in Figure 2.15. He selected five functions and then wrote the task statements shown in Figure 2.16.

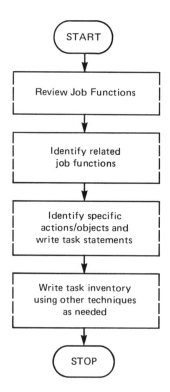

Figure 2.14. Job Function Technique.

JOB FUNCTION	DESCRIPTION
Information Functions	
Comparing	Selecting, sorting, classifying, arranging, and assigning data, people, or things using a prescribed system.
Copying	Writing, typing, copying, transcribing, entering and/or posting data using a variety of work aids following a specific plan.
Computing	Performing arithmetic operations to complete actions or reports.
Compiling	Collecting, gathering, classifying, and compiling information using a discretionary system.
Analyzing	Check, examine, and evaluate information using standards to determine effects and alternatives.
Innovating	Modify, alter, or adapt existing information to meet changing standards or conditions.
Coordinating	Set goals and standards; decide time, place, and sequence of goal-related activities; oversee actions, and report results.
Synthesizing	Conceive new approaches, designs, solutions, or developments which are outside existing ideas based on intuitions, feelings, or ideas.
People Functions	
Instruction taking-helping	Follow assignments, instructions, or orders without verbal exchange beyond clarification of the instruction.
Serving	Immediately responding to the needs or requests of people or animals.
Exchanging Information	Talking and signaling people to obtain or clarify information to follow established procedures.
Coaching	Helping, instructing, advising, and encouraging people in a caring one-on-one or small group setting.

Figure 2.15. Standard Listing of Job Functions.

JOB FUNCTION	DESCRIPTION
Persuading	Selling or influencing others to favor a product, service, or point of view.
Diverting	Amusing, entertaining, or distracting people
Consulting	Defining, providing, clarifying, or improving information, procedures, or performance to help people as requested.
Instructing	Teaching or training people or animals.
Treating	Observing, prescribing, treating, and interacting with people or animals to adjust health (sickness) or behavior.
Supervising	Defining and interpreting procedures, assigning duties, and evaluating performance to promote efficiency and a harmonious setting.
Negotiating	Representing people to formally discuss and bargain advantages in resources, rights, privileges, or obligations.
Mentoring	Diagnosing, counseling, advising, and guiding people to improve life adjustment.
Things Functions	
Handling	Working, assembling, digging, moving, or carrying one or a few objects using relatively gross precision.
Feeding-Offbearing	Inserting, throwing, dumping, or placing into, or removing objects from equipment which is automatic or tended by others. Precision requirements built into the machinery.
Tending	Starting, monitoring, and stopping equipment with highly prescribed adjustment and little nonstandard performance that is set up by other workers and involves adjusting controls in response to automatic signals.
Manipulating	Working, assembling, digging, moving, guiding, or placing several objects using a variety of precision requirements.

Figure 2.15 (Continued)

JOB FUNCTION	DESCRIPTION
Operating-Controlling	Readying, starting, controlling, monitoring, or adjusting machinery or equipment to fabricate or process data, people, or things.
Driving-Controlling	Starting, steering, guiding, controlling, and stopping machines to process and move people or things.
Precision Working	Working, moving, guiding, or placing objects or materials according to standard procedures of an entire craft to precise tolerances as is done with power or manual hand tools.
Setting Up	Installing, inserting, altering, troubleshooting, repairing, or restoring equipment to meet job specifications.

Figure 2.15 (Continued)

SELECTED JOB FUNCTION	TASK STATEMENTS
Information Functions	
Compiling	Write lesson plans Write student handouts Write tests
Analyzing	Grade tests Evaluate trainees' performance
Coordinating	Schedule courses Plan equipment usage Report student progress
People Functions	
Instructing	Teach people to drive forklift Teach people to control crane Teach people to control trackmobile
Things Functions	
Driving-Controlling	Drive forklift Control crane Control trackmobile

Figure 2.16. Job Function Analysis

RISK ASSESSMENT TECHNIQUE

Purpose

The Risk Assessment Technique is used after the task inventory is compiled to determine the *importance* and *difficulty* of each task. From this assessment the analyst can target selected tasks for further analysis and training.

Advantages

This technique allows the analyst to sort difficult and important tasks from easy and unimportant tasks, thus reducing the amount of analysis and training development time required. Costs associated with analysis and training development are also reduced.

Disadvantages

Since the response of various individuals is usually used to assess the importance and difficulty of the tasks, uninformed opinion may dilute the accuracy of the results. Some important tasks may be eliminated from further analysis and eventual training. If this occurs, the costs associated with the resulting poor performance could increase.

Description

The analyst uses master performers' ratings of task criticality to determine the need for continued analysis. This process is flow-charted in Figure 2.17 and uses the following steps:

1. Select rating factors and add them to the task inventory (see example in Figure 2.19). The two most important rating factors are difficulty and importance. The *difficulty* factor assesses the chance of performance error by asking the following question: "What is the possibility of inadequate performance from the average employee?" The difficulty factor can be scaled in the following way:

    (1) *Very Low*—Very little chance of error, among the easiest 10 percent of all tasks.

    (2) *Low*—Little chance of error, easier than average but not among the easiest, easier than 7 out of 10 tasks.

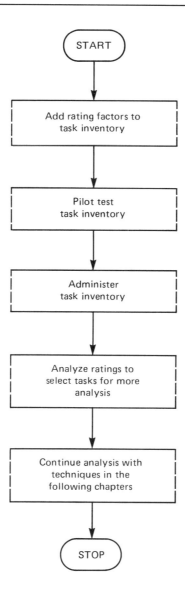

Figure 2.17. Risk Assessment Technique.

(3) *Moderate*—Some chance of error, difficulty is average.

(4) *High*—Error is likely, harder than average but not among the most difficult, more difficult than 7 out of 10 tasks.

(5) *Very High*—Error almost certain, harder than 90 percent of all tasks.

The second factor, *importance*, assumes that performance error is made and assesses the cost of error by asking the following question: "What is the cost to safety, lost revenue, and public relations if the task is performed inadequately?"

The importance factor can be scaled in the following way:

(1) *Very Low*—Inadequate performance makes almost no difference.

(2) *Low*—Inadequate performance has undesirable public relations consequences, but the consequences are not too costly, and are not unsafe.

(3) *Moderate*—Inadequate performance has serious public relations consequences which are quite costly, and affect safety.

(4) *High*—Inadequate performance has severe public relations consequences which are very costly, and are quite dangerous.

(5) *Very High*—Inadequate performance has extremely severe public relations consequences which are enormously time-consuming or costly, and are very dangerous.

Other factors may be used to describe the task. These factors are less important to deciding if analysis should continue, but may help during further analysis and training development. For instance, the frequency of performance is often assessed. However, this factor does not affect criticality. The most critical tasks of jobs like airplane pilots or nuclear power plant operators are infrequently performed.

Frequent tasks may or may not be important or difficult. Task frequency becomes important, however, when considering retraining, since frequently performed tasks do not require retraining if performance is adequate. The following factors may be included during risk assessment to collect information for future use:

(1) Relative time spent on the task (very much above average, above average, slightly above average, about average, slightly below average, below average, very much below average).

(2) Actual time spent on the task.

(3) Frequency of performance (day, week, month, year).

(4) Special training required.

(5) Learning difficulty.

(6) Supervision required.

(7) Satisfaction gained from performance.

(8) Performer characteristics.

2. Pilot test the task inventory by having several individuals rate and review the task statements and selected factors. Revise the task inventory to eliminate problem areas.

3. Send task inventories to the selected audience and have them rate all tasks. With large audiences, special mark-sensing forms can be used to facilitate later computer processing.

   Selecting a proper audience is often a problem. If true master performers are available, it is possible to get correct responses from two to five individuals. However, it is often difficult to identify true master performers, so it is better to use the total population (for small audiences) or to use sample raters (for large audiences). The following sampling procedures may be used:

   Random Sampling—Determine the size of the population and use a random number generator to select raters.

   Stratified Sampling—Categorize the population into separate groups, i.e., length of time in the position, pay grade, geographical location, or type of equipment used. Then, randomly select a certain number of raters from each category. With very large populations a sample of 400 is usually optimum. Stratified sampling makes it possible to compare the responses of different types of master performers or novices—an important consideration when designing training.

4. Analyze the ratings and select those tasks that require further analysis and training. The tasks can be sorted according to difficulty and importance as shown in Figure 2.18. The ratings can be interpreted in the following ways:

   (1) *Very Difficult and Important*—These are the most critical tasks. High importance means that analysis should continue and include equipment and job redesign and the development of job aids. High difficulty means that employees will probably require training in a simulated environment where consequences are lower.

   (2) *Very Difficult but Not Important*—These tasks have high difficulty so training is probably required. However, since the importance is low, the training can usually be done in the workplace or on-the-job. Continuing the analysis to develop job aids is useful but may not be required.

   (3) *Moderately Difficult and Important*—These tasks are quite critical. Analysis should result in job aids. The lower difficulty implies less demanding training, but a safe simulated environment like a classroom is still desirable.

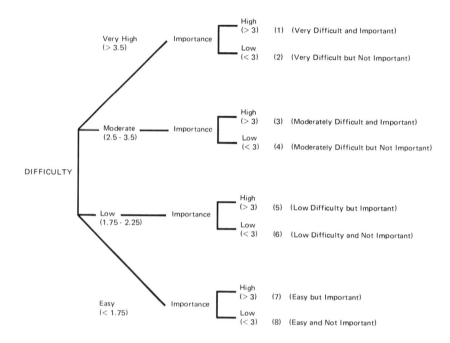

Figure 2.18. Task Selection Decision Tree.

(4) *Moderately Difficult but Not Important*—Formal training is not demanded for these tasks, but it is still desirable. Low importance implies that the training can be done safely in the workplace or on-the-job. Additional analysis might be needed to organize on-the-job training.

(5) *Low Difficulty but Important*—These tasks require little formal training because of low difficulty. High importance, however, demands that analysis continues to redesign the job or produce job aids so that serious consequences associated with the unlikely error are reduced as much as possible.

(6) *Low Difficulty and Not Important*—Little training or job redesign is required of these tasks so analysis stops. On-the-job familiariza-tion is usually adequate.

(7) *Easy but Important*—Training is almost never required for these tasks, but the slight possibility of error results in serious consequences so analysis might continue to redesign jobs and job aids.

(8) *Easy and Not Important*—These tasks do not require further analysis or training.

5. Continue analysis for those tasks which need it using the techniques discussed in the chapters which follow.

Example

Figure 2.19 summarizes the ratings of ten nuclear power plant operators on a portion of a task inventory. All five task statements for the control rod drive system were determined to be part of the job. The ratings for each task were averaged. For instance, Figure 2.20 shows that the mean rating for task 1.2 (start rod drive motor) is 1.8 (difficulty) and 4.4 (importance). Using the task selection decision tree (Figure 2.18), it was determined that analysis of task 1.2 should continue to the development of job aids. Training, however, is not required.

Task No.	Task	Never Done	Difficulty					Importance				
			Very low	Low	Moderate	High	Very high	Very low	Low	Moderate	High	Very high
			1	2	3	4	5	1	2	3	4	5
1.0	Control Rod Drive System											
1.1	Monitor rod drive system indications	0	0	0	1	3	6	0	1	1	4	4
1.2	Start rod drive motor	0	4	5	0	1	0	0	0	1	4	5
1.3	Stop rod drive motor	0	6	3	1	0	0	7	2	1	0	0
1.4	Monitor static inverter	0	0	0	2	7	1	5	5	0	0	0
1.5	Take rod drive motor vibration readings	0	0	3	6	1	0	0	0	7	3	0

Figure 2.19. Complete Task Inventory.

Task No.	Task	Mean Diffi- Culty	Mean Impor- tance	Decision
1.1	Monitor rod drive system indications	4.5	4.5	Continue analysis, job and equipment redesign, job aids, training
1.2	Start rod drive motor	1.8	4.4	Continue analysis, job aids, no training
1.3	Stop rod drive motor	1.5	1.4	No further analysis or training
1.4	Monitor static	3.9	1.5	Only analyze to on-the-job training require-ments
1.5	Take rod drive motor vibration readings	2.8	3.3	Continue analysis, job and equipment redesign, job aids, training if necessary

Figure 2.20. Task Inventory Interpretation.

Chapter Summary

One important part of analyzing a job or task is identifying what the job or task is. The analyst writes task statements which describe the job. Task statements are simple sentences with a concrete action and object that describe job activities. Task statements can be identified using the Interview Note Technique, Card-Sort Technique, Task Matrix Technique, List Expansion Technique, Daily Log Technique, Walk and Talk Technique, or Job Function Technique. The Risk Assessment Technique is then used to evaluate the need for further analysis of each task statement.

The various techniques can often be used interchangeably, but

SITUATION	SUGGESTED TECHNIQUE
Job related documentation does not exist and master performers are the sole informa- tion source, or task statements need addi- tional detailing and it is felt that the detailing process must be very controlled (perhaps because master performers will not take the required time).	Interview Note Technique
Job related documentation exists, but the task statements must be identified, written, and reordered.	Card-Sort Technique
Task statements are identified and a general level task breakdown is desired.	Task Matrix Technique
Task statements are identified and a detailed task breakdown is desired.	List Expansion Technique
Job consists of many activities which are difficult to identify precisely (managerial and supervisory jobs).	Daily Log Technique
The job consists of so many activities, and related equipment, that it is difficult to remember them all during an interview.	Walk and Talk Technique
It is helpful to contrast the job against standardized work classifications to ensure that all areas are taken into account.	Job Function Technique
The need for additional analysis must be assessed.	Risk Assessment Technique

Figure 2.21. Finding What the Job Is Techniques Summary.

their advantages and disadvantages make it possible to suggest the best technique for a given situation. These suggestions are summarized in Figure 2.21.

Once the analyst has determined what the job is by completing a task inventory, it is often necessary to analyze *how* critical tasks are done. This is the subject of the next chapter.

3

Finding How the Job Is Done

Once the analyst has discovered what tasks are significant and has a list of task statements, it is important to describe how the tasks are done. The tasks are analyzed for sequence, relationship, and other details like needed tools, equipment, and materials. A detailed task description takes a great amount of time and effort, so *it is usually only done for the most critical tasks.*

Main Goal: To Detail and Sequence Task Statements

When describing "how" a task is done, the analyst details each critical task statement and shows the sequence followed. Typically, the master performer is observed while doing the task. He or she is also asked to describe what is being done. The analyst lists each detail performed and described, along with the order of performance. From the listing, it is possible to develop job aids and training programs.

The techniques used to describe "how" a task is done include the Basic Task Description Technique, the Stimulus-Response Chart Technique, the Process Chart Technique, the Operation Chart Technique, the Man-Machine Time Chart Technique, the Flow Chart Technique, and the Picture Technique. Each of these seven techniques will be described in this chapter.

BASIC TASK DESCRIPTION TECHNIQUE

Purpose
The Basic Task Description Technique is used to record the steps or elements in a task along with related information like conditions, equipment, and standards.

Advantages
The Basic Task Description Technique works best on sequential step-by-step type tasks requiring a moderate level of detail. The background information on conditions, equipment, standards, references, etc., which is collected is valuable for training program development.

Disadvantages
Tasks which involve multiple decisions using various data inputs, non-sequential elements, or a very detailed level of description are not easily recorded using the Basic Task Description Technique. The completed task descriptions, although very useful for creating training, do not serve well as job aids or learning aids.

Description
The analyst collects detailed information about task steps. This process is flow-charted in Figure 3.1 and uses the following steps:
1. Select the data categories which are important to the task being described. Different jobs will require different categories because of variety in equipment, conditions, or activities. The following categories have often been used during task description:
    - *Task Element*—A discrete action, step, or subtask executed during task performance. This category is required for all analyses.
    - *Element Number*—The sequential number assigned to each task element.
    - *Task Conditions*—The environmental conditions, information, and resources that are requisite to the performance.
    - *Initiating Cue*—The initial stimulus that prompts performance of the entire task.
    - *Stimulus*—The prerequisites or cues that cause the performance of each individual element. These are the initiating cues for each individual task element.
    - *Instructions*—The spoken directions given to the performer by others while the task is being done.

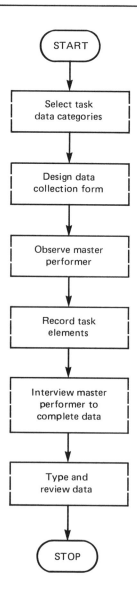

Figure 3.1. Basic Task Description Technique.

- *References*—The procedures, manuals, and technical materials used to perform each task element.
- *Tools and Equipment*—The tools and equipment that are used during performance, i.e., gloves, calculator, microcomputer, hammer.
- *Devices (Displays) and Location*—The specific parts, switches, or individual controls used while performing, and their location on the equipment.
- *Control Action*—A description of the action required when manipulating the device or display, i.e., turn clockwise, push up, pull out one inch.
- *Indication*—The observable result from manipulating a control, switch, part, etc.
- *Standards*—The limits, specifications, tolerances, or time requirements which must be adhered to during the performance.
- *Safety Factors*—The steps that must be followed to ensure that the element is performed safely.
- *Problem Assessment*—The problems that are likely to occur while performing the element. Each statement should begin with "What if . . .?" as shown in the following examples:
  —What if the switch fails to work?
  —What if the oil is too heavy?
- *Problem Resolution*—The most likely resolution to each problem identified during problem assessment.
- *Terminating Cue*—The indication or cue that tells when the task is complete.
- *Output*—The final results, stated in measurable terms, which are anticipated from the task. These include indications of task accomplishment and consumer satisfaction.
- *Task Evaluation*—The measurable requirements against which performance could be evaluated. These include indications of quantity and quality (accuracy, completeness, cost, timeliness, safety).
- *Consequence of Inadequate Performance*—The potential effects on public relations, equipment, costs, and safety from incorrect performance.
- *Human Interfaces*—The position titles and basic responsibilities of personnel with whom the worker interfaces during the performance.
- *Skills and Knowledges*—The information and abilities required while performing each task element. These should be written at a moderate level of detail. Terms like "purpose of," "familiarity with," and "relationship to" are not sufficient. A short description

of the purpose or relationship is required. However, specific values and formulas are too detailed and need not be included.

2. Design a data collection form. The column format is frequently used. Example formats are shown in Figure 3.2.

3. Observe master performers while they do each task. It is helpful to videotape the master performer if this does not interfere too much with task performance.

4. Record all task elements in the appropriate column on the data collection form. This is done by writing short task statements which complete the questions "first you . . .?, then you . . .?, then you . . .?," etc. For instance, for the task "change car tire" the following elements might be recorded:

    First you—Remove jack from trunk.
    Then you—Remove spare tire from trunk.
    Then you—Place jack under frame.
    Then you—Raise car weight off tire.
    Then you—Loosen lug nuts.
    Then you—Raise car so tire leaves ground.
    Then you—Remove lug nuts.
    Then you—Remove flat tire.
    Then you—Put on spare tire.
    Then you—Tighten lug nuts.
    Then you—Lower car.
    Then you—Retighten lug nuts.
    Then you—Place flat tire in trunk.
    Then you—Place jack in trunk.

5. Interview the master performer to get information needed to complete each of the selected categories. Figure 3.3 shows a completed data collection form.

6. Type and review data collection forms to ensure correctness.

Example

One task of the radiation technician at a nuclear power plant is to source-check radiation detectors to ensure they are working properly. While analyzing this task to determine how it is done, the analyst completed the data collection form shown in Figure 3.3. The categories on this form (device, control, indication) were selected to match this particular task. A master performer was observed and the basic task elements identified. An interview with the master performer was then conducted to complete the chart. After being typed, the form received a final review by the master performer to ensure correctness.

JOB POSITION:		TASK:	
ELEMENT #	TASK ELEMENT	STIMULUS	STANDARD

JOB POSITION:		TASK:			
TASK ELEMENT	DEVICE/ LOCATION	CONTROL ACTION	INDI- CATION	PROBLEM ASSESSMENT	PROBLEM RESOLUTION

JOB POSITION:		TASK:		
TASK ELEMENT	HUMAN INTERFACES	REFERENCES	TOOLS/ EQUIPMENT	SKILLS/ KNOWLEDGES

Figure 3.2. Formats for Data Collection Form.

JOB POSITION: Radiation Technician			TASK: Source Check Radiation Detector		
TASK ELEMENT	DEVICE/ LOCATION	CONTROL ACTION	INDICATION	PROBLEM ASSESSMENT	PROBLEM RESOLUTION
1. Take detector off shelf	Detector cabinet	Carry			
2. Check detector appearance	Cable, probe, case, handle, nobs	Visual Inspection		What if parts are broken, missing, or loose?	Place reject sticker on detector.
3. Set response time	Toggle switch, right front	Push down to slow position	Indication needle swings slowly (11 secs.) when placed by radiation source		
4. Turn on audio	Toggle switch, middle front	Push down to on position	Clicking sound when placed by radiation source		
5. Check battery	Nob, left front	Turn left one click	Battery needle swings to test area	What if needle does not reach test area?	Replace battery and recheck
6. Get radiation source	Source cabinet	Carry		What if radiation is too high?	No high source radiation available
7. Set level indicator	Nob, left front	Turn left on setting required by radiation source	Needle will swing when placed by radiation source	What if needle does not swing?	Place reject sticker on detector
8. Determine detector radiation response	Needle, top front	Automatic	Swings slowly from left to right and gives scale reading equal to source	What if needle does not swing? What if scale reading is wrong?	Place reject sticker on detector
9. Return radiation source	Source Cabinet	Carry			
10. Return detector to shelve	Detector Cabinet	Carry			

Figure 3.3. Completed Basic Task Description.

STIMULUS-RESPONSE CHART TECHNIQUE

Purpose
The Stimulus-Response Chart Technique is used to describe task steps in great detail. It is important when the tasks are very complex, involving numerous people, data inputs, or decisions.

Advantages
With the Stimulus-Response Chart Technique, each individual action is related to an initiating stimulus. This technique is very useful with complex tasks which involve multiple inputs and responses. It is also valuable as a short-hand technique for formatting many task statements on a single sequence chart.

Disadvantages
The Stimulus-Response Chart is often difficult for novice analysts and trainees to understand. Therefore, it is seldom a good job aid.

Description
The analyst records the stimulus which leads to each detailed step and the response that follows. This process is flow-charted in Figure 3.4 and includes the following steps:

1. Observe a master performer doing the task. List the basic sequence of actions performed. Alternatives to this step include videotaping the performance or locating a previously prepared task description or procedure.

2. Meet with the master performer and review the task listing. With the master performer's help, chart the actual performance on a stimulus-response chart. This chart shows each stimulus (S) or initiating cue and its corresponding performance action response (R). For example, the stimulus "telephone rings" initiates the response "answer the telephone," which is charted as follows:

S ————————————— R
Telephone Rings   Answer Telephone

Simple jobs involve single chains of the stimulus-response pairs, while complex jobs involve decisions or discriminations, groupings or generalizations, and other complex combinations (see the example in Figure 3.6).

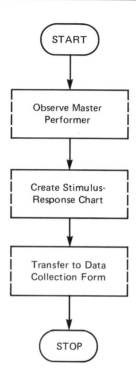

Figure 3.4. Stimulus-Response Chart Technique.

These various possibilities are charted with the following conventions:

a. Stimulus-response pairs are separated with dots to form a chain or logical sequence with no decision points. The behavior is charted in this way whenever the stimulus is always the same, and when the performer always responds in the same way.

$$S \text{———} R \bullet S \text{———} R \bullet S \text{———} R$$

b. Discriminations are preceded by a vertical line. A discrimination is a decision that requires different responses to two or more related stimuli. Discriminations may not be observed during a single observation of everyday performance. They are discovered by probing and asking the master performer "What other stimuli might occur at this point?" or "What problems could occur at this point?"

```
                    | S ———————— R
S ———— R • | S ———————— R • S ———— R
                    | S ———————— R
```

c. Generalizations are single responses to multiple stimuli and are indicated using forked lines. Generalizations also may not be observed in everyday performance. They are discovered by asking "What other stimuli could occur at this point that would result in the same response?"

```
              S ———
S ———— R •  S ——————  R • S ———— R
              S ———
```

d. Multiple responses to a single stimulus are preceded by a vertical line and followed by another vertical line or dots depending upon the next stimulus in the sequence. Multiple responses could be done in any order; however, each must eventually be followed to an end point.

```
          | R |                | R • S ———— R
S ———— | R | • S ———— | R • S ———— R
          | R |                | R • S ———— R
```

e. Continuing a chain of S-R connections from one *place* to another on the same page is done using circled letters.

```
          S ———— R • S ———— R • S ———— R  (A)
(A)      S ———— R • S ———— R
```

f. Continuing a chain of S-R connections from one *page* to another page is done using letters and numbers in pointed boxes.

```
Page 1    S ———— R • S ———— R • S ———— R   [A3 >
Page 3  [1A >      S ———— R • S ———— R
```

g. Completion of a path is indicated using the symbol "(end)."

h. A stimulus which begins a sequence is indicated using the symbol " * ".

i. Responses are all individually numbered in brackets (see (1) (2) (3) in Figure 3.5). Numbering begins with the first response and follows the uppermost path until an (End) is reached. Then numbering begins with the next lower discrimination path with an unnumbered response, etc., until all pathways are numbered.

3. Transfer the charted information to a data collection form. This makes the information easier to understand. This step is often not done if the task is very simple, but complex tasks are more easily understood when put in the data collection format. Figure 3.5 shows how the charted information is

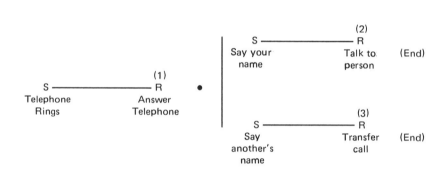

ELEMENT #	ELEMENTS	CONDITIONS
1 (2,3)	Answer Telephone	Telephone Rings
2 (End)	Talk to Person	Say Your Name
3 (End)	Transfer Call	Say Another's Name

Figure 3.5. Stimulus-Response Chart and Data Collection Form.

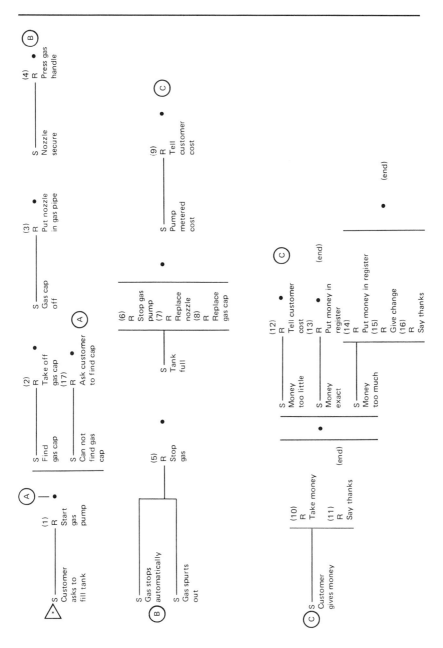

Figure 3.6. Filling Gas Tank Stimulus-Response Chart.

JOB POSITION: Service Station Attendant TASK: 1 - Fill gas tank		
ELEMENT #	ELEMENT	CONDITIONS
1 (2,17)	Start gas pump	Customer asks to fill gas tank
2 (3)	Take off gas cap	Finds gas cap
3 (4)	Put nozzle in gas pipe	Gas cap off
4 (5)	Press gas handle	Nozzle secure
5 (6,7,8)	Stop gas nozzle	Gas stops automatically or gas spurts out
6 (9)	Stop gas pump	Tank full
7 (9)	Replace nozzle	Tank full
8 (9)	Replace gas cap	Tank full
9 (10-11)	Tell customer cost	Pump metered cost
10 (12-16)	Take money	Customer gives money
11 (End)	Say thank you	Customer gives money
12 (10-11)	Tell customer cost	Money too little
13 (End)	Put money in register	Money just right
14 (End)	Put money in register	Money too much
15 (End)	Give change	Money too much
16 (End)	Say thank you	Money too much
17 (2)	Ask customer to show cap	Cannot find gas cap

Figure 3.7. Filling Gas Tank Data Collection Form.

transferred. The charted response number one (1) was placed in the "Element #" space along with the next responses to which it leads (numbers in brackets). The response "Answer Telephone" was placed in the "Element" column, and the stimulus "Telephone Rings" was placed in the "Conditions" column.

Example

One of the tasks of a service station employee is to fill gas tanks. A master performer at filling tanks was observed and the stimulus-response chart in Figure 3.6 was created. After the stimulus-response chart was complete, the information was transferred to the data collection form in Figure 3.7.

PROCESS CHART TECHNIQUE

Purpose

The Process Chart Technique is used to record and categorize the steps in a task. Five basic task categories are used to give a fairly simple description of the task. From the finished chart, improvements can be made to the process.

Advantages

The Process Chart Technique has two principal advantages: (1) the information is recorded in a short, concise manner and (2) the steps are categorized so needed improvements can be identified. Also, when workers interact on the job, their activities can be recorded on the same chart. This technique is useful for improving jobs where routing and travel time are critical.

Disadvantages

Complex decisions and groupings are not easily recorded with the Process Chart Technique. It is best for basic, linear tasks like those found in assembly line jobs.

Description

The analyst categorizes and records the basic process which the master performer uses when doing the task. This process is flow-charted in Figure 3.8 and uses the following steps:

1. Design the process chart to match the type of task being analyzed. A process chart always has chart symbols and a process description. It may also include time, distance, group-work, and summary sections. Figures 3.9, 3.10, and 3.11 show process chart formats for an individual process, a group or team process, and a multi-task process.

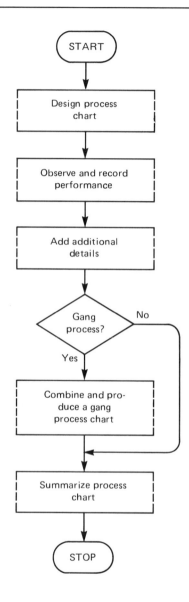

Figure 3.8. Process Chart Technique.

Process chart symbols are used during data collection as a short-hand method for categorizing and recording the steps in the task. The following symbols are used:

Operation—The object is changed in one or more character- istics, i.e., assembled, disassembled, changed physically or chemically, or rearranged.

Transportation—The object is moved, or the person moves from one place to another.

Inspection—The object is identified or examined against a standard of quality or quantity.

Delay—The object or process is retained or delayed while waiting for the next step.

Storage—The object is kept under control until removal is authorized.

2. Observe and record the performance. Each chart symbol is usually identified first, then the process description is completed. As can be seen in Figure 3.12, the symbols are identified and sequenced with a connecting line and the process description is either a short task statement, an indication of where transporation or storage is, or a description of the inspection standard.

3. Observe and record other needed information. Several observations may be required to ensure that the process is correctly described, and to add details like distances moved or time used.

4. Combine process charts when different individuals give input to the process. A gang process chart is made like the example in Figures 3.10 and 3.11. This chart shows the interrelationships between all workers and the process.

5. Summarize the process chart. The summary should include the total number of operations, transportations, inspections, and delays, as well as other data, i.e., total distance traveled, and total time used. After the summary is complete, the task can be analyzed and restructured to eliminate unneeded delay or travel. This analysis and restructuring will be discussed in greater detail in the next chapter of this text.

DISTANCE IN FEET	TIME IN MINUTES	CHART SYMBOL	PROCESS DESCRIPTION
	15		First step
10	1		Second step
	5		Third step
	2		Fourth step

Figure 3.9. Individual Process Chart Format.

1st person	2nd person	3rd person	4th person	5th person	6th person	7th person	8th person	9th person	10th person	PROCESS DESCRIPTION
										First step
										Second step
										Third step
										Fourth step

Figure 3.10. Gang Process Chart Format.

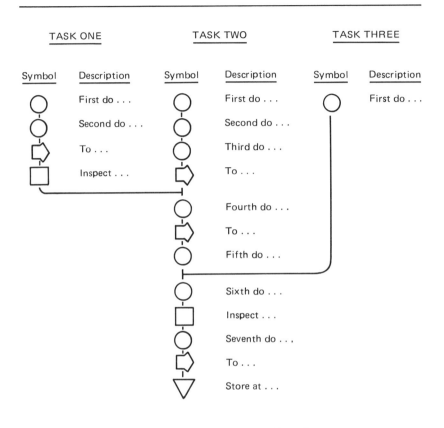

Figure 3.11. Multi-Task Process Chart Format.

Example

Completing the attendance sheet is an important task for instructors. A process chart was made for this task (Figure 3.12). The specific class observed had 14 students. After the process was charted the summary was completed by adding all the different process symbols.

Subject: Completion of training attendance form   Date   3/1/84
Beginning Point: Instructor starts one-day course
Ending Point: Instructor submits records for filing

CHART SYMBOLS	PROCESS DESCRIPTION
◯	Course name and date written by instructor
⇨	to student
◯	student signs name
⇨	to next student
◯	next student signs name
	Previous two steps continue until all 14 students have signed.
D	on back desk
☐	instructor collects attendance sheet and examines
◯	instructor signs approval
D	waits for other records and test grades
⇨	to file clerk
▽	form filed.

SUMMARY: Includes all 14 students

Operations ◯		16
Transportations ⇨		15
Inspections ☐		1
Delays D		2
Storages ▽		1

Figure 3.12. Attendance Form Process Chart.

OPERATION CHART TECHNIQUE

Purpose

The Operation Chart Technique is used to record, categorize, and improve the detailed motions and senses involved in skilled jobs.

Advantages

The Operation Chart Technique records very detailed motions used during performance. The senses may also be charted. The motions and senses are categorized so that different ways of doing a task can be compared easily.

Disadvantages

The Operation Chart Technique works best with sequential, detailed tasks. Complex decisions are not easily charted. This type of analysis is very costly because of the time required to record details. The work environment may be disrupted since hours are often spent literally looking over the worker's shoulder. Videotaping the performance can help reduce disruptions and reduce the disadvantages associated with this technique.

Description

The analyst records the detailed motions and senses used in the task. This process is flow-charted in Figure 3.13 and uses the following steps:

1. Design the operation chart to match the task being analyzed. The chart may have columns for left hand, right hand, type of activity, senses (sight, smell), time, additional comments, etc. The chart should include as *few columns as needed* to reduce data collection.
2. Observe and record the performance on the chart. Initial recording is usually abbreviated and rough.
3. Immediately interview the master performer to clarify actions and add comments.
4. Categorize each activity. One simple scheme uses two symbols. A small circle indicates transportation, such as moving a hand to pick up something, and a large circle indicates operations like grasping, pressing, or positioning. Other, more complex, categories have been used in detailed job studies (see SIMO chart in Barnes, 1980, in references section).
5. Summarize the activities by adding the categories for each hand.
6. Produce a finished chart. The chart is very useful during the creation of training programs. The finished chart is organized spatially with right and left hand columns to help eye movements while reading and learning the activities. The next chapter (Path Analysis Technique) contains a discussion of how the Process Operation Chart can be used to improve the job.

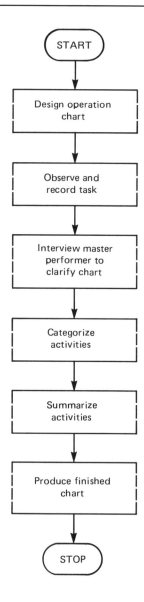

Figure 3.13. Operation Chart Technique.

Example

Instructional media producers often use the Kroy brand lettering machine to produce lettering for posters, slides, and transparencies. A master performer at this task was observed and the use of left hand, right hand, and senses was recorded on an operation chart. Following the observation, an interview was conducted to complete the operation chart and categorize the activities. The finished chart of this task is shown in Figure 3.14. The master performer used seven operations and one transportation with the right hand, and seven operations and three transportations with the left hand.

TASK: Produce Lettering on a Kroy Lettering Machine

LEFT HAND	ACTIVITY		RIGHT HAND	SENSES	COMMENTS
				Look at first word on paper	
				Inspect location of letter wheel	
Place thumb on 0 control (hand resting on side of machine, wrist resting on table).	0	0	Grasp center of letter wheel (fingers spread across top, thumb at bottom).		
		0	Turn letter wheel in shortest direction to desired letter (move only fingers and thumb, no wrist or arm movement.	Inspect letter wheel	
Press thumb lightly and quickly let up (only move thumb).	0	0 0	Briefly release grasp on letter wheel, then regrasp.		Releasing grasp allows wheel to center on letter.
		0	Turn letter wheel in shortest direction to next desired letter.	Inspect letter wheel	
Press thumb lightly and quickly let up. (repeat)	0		(repeat)	(repeat)	Continue iterating the preceding process until all words are complete.
		0	Turn wheel shortest distance to advance	Inspect location	
Move thumb one inch to left.	•				
Press arrow control.	0			Inspect tape length	If tape is too short, press control again.
Move entire arm up one inch.	•				
Place thumb on scissor control and press firmly.	0			Inspect cut	If tape not cut press scissor control again.
Pick up tape with thumb and first finger, move arm one foot left to container, and release tape.	0 • 0	0 •	Release letter wheel and move hand to side.		
TOTAL	• =3 0=7	• =1 0=7			

Figure 3.14. Example Operation Chart.

MAN-MACHINE TIME CHART TECHNIQUE

Purpose

The Man-Machine Time Chart Technique is used when time is important to the analysis, and a man (or woman) interacts during the performance with an operating machine.

Advantages

The Man-Machine Time Chart Technique is used to analyze the relationships of time, the worker's activities, and the machine's activities. The relationships which are described give a better understanding of the task so it can be re-designed to save time and other resources.

Disadvantages

The Man-Machine Time Chart Technique works best with sequential tasks. Complex decisions are not easily charted. This detailed analysis is quite costly. As with any detailed observation, the work environment is easily disrupted.

Description

The analyst charts the interface between the performer, the machine used, and the time spent on the task. This process is flow-charted in Figure 3.15 and uses the following steps:

1. Design the man-machine time chart to match the task being analyzed. The chart may have multiple columns for various operators or machines. There is always a running time scale and an individual time column for each operator and machine. Figure 3.16 shows some possible man-machine time chart formats.
2. Observe, time, and record the performance. Several observations are usually needed to collect all necessary data to ensure that all steps are listed and that the average or mean times for each step are identified.
3. Produce the initial chart. The initial observations are clarified, rewritten, and carefully recorded in a near final form.
4. Check the chart by observing the performance once more to ensure that it is correct.
5. Revise as needed and produce the final man-machine time chart.

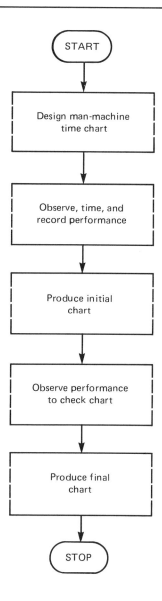

Figure 3.15. Man-Machine Time Chart Technique.

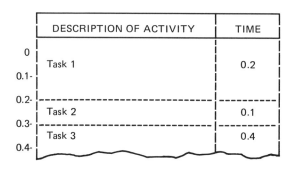

	DESCRIPTION OF ACTIVITY	TIME
0	Task 1	0.2
0.1-		
0.2-	Task 2	0.1
0.3-	Task 3	0.4
0.4-		

	OPERATOR	TIME	MACHINE	TIME
0-			Idle	1
1-	Task 1	2		
2-	Idle	1	Task 1	6
3-				
4-	Task 2	2		
5-				

	OPERATOR	TIME	HELPER	TIME	MACHINE	TIME
0	Task 1	1			Idle	1
1-	Task 2	2	Idle	2		
2-			Task 1	1	Task 1	3
3-						
4-	Idle	3	Task 2	3	Task 2	2

Figure 3.16. Man-Machine Time Chart Formats.

Example

Figure 3.17 shows a completed man-machine time chart for the task of cleaning and drying laundry. The chart has columns for one operator and two machines (washer, dryer). Task performance was observed and basic notes on tasks and times were taken. Then the analyst created an initial chart. The initial chart was revised as a result of a second comparative observation, and the final man-machine time chart (Figure 3.17) was produced.

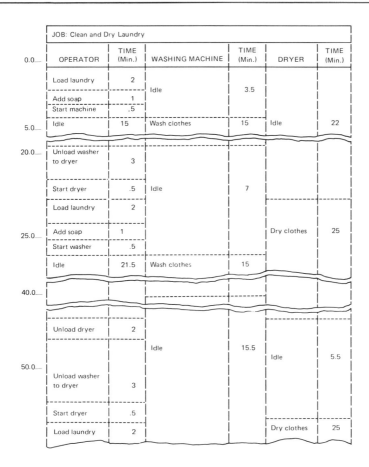

	OPERATOR	TIME (Min.)	WASHING MACHINE	TIME (Min.)	DRYER	TIME (Min.)
0.0	Load laundry	2	Idle	3.5		
	Add soap	1				
	Start machine	.5				
5.0	Idle	15	Wash clothes	15	Idle	22
20.0	Unload washer to dryer	3				
	Start dryer	.5	Idle	7		
	Load laundry	2				
25.0	Add soap	1			Dry clothes	25
	Start washer	.5				
	Idle	21.5	Wash clothes	15		
40.0						
	Unload dryer	2				
			Idle	15.5	Idle	5.5
50.0	Unload washer to dryer	3				
	Start dryer	.5				
	Load laundry	2			Dry clothes	25

JOB: Clean and Dry Laundry

Figure 3.17. Man-Machine Time Chart of Laundry Task.

FLOW CHART TECHNIQUE

Purpose

The Flow Chart Technique is used to show the sequential actions and decisions in a complex process. It reduces complexity by showing a likely set of actions and simple decisions.

Advantages

The Flow Chart Technique is relatively simple to use and produces a very clear and understandable task description. Alternative actions are shown as sequential steps. Logical inconsistencies in the task are identified. This method is reasonably time efficient. The finished chart is a valuable job and learning aid.

Disadvantages

Drawing and revising flow charts can prove more costly than prose descriptions. Flow charts with detailed descriptions are lengthy. Jobs with many-option decisions are not handled easily with the Flow Chart Technique.

Description

The analyst flow-charts the steps in the process and the decisions that are made. This process is shown in Figure 3.18 and uses the following steps:

1. Develop a basic behavior path showing *only* the actions representing the *most likely* performance flow. Each behavior description begins with an action word, is usually less than ten words long, and is written in a rectangular box. Sequential boxes are connected with arrows. The path can be developed from observation, but it is usually easier to have a small group of master performers brainstorm the actions until consensus is reached on the most likely flow. While brainstorming, the flow path boxes can be drawn on a sheet of paper, but with a group of master performers it is easier to write each behavior on a 3 x 5 card and post the cards on a large wall. This makes it easier for all to see the brainstormed steps and to revise the flow.

2. Identify contingencies which might be performed. These contingencies should be written as a question with a simple yes or no answer. These decision questions might ask if a particular event occurred, if a standard has been met, or if a process is complete. Decision questions are written in diamond shapes. Cut-down 3 x 5 cards (3 x 3) serve for decision shapes when brainstorming and posting cards on a wall. The decision questions should be inserted where they occur in the basic flow path.

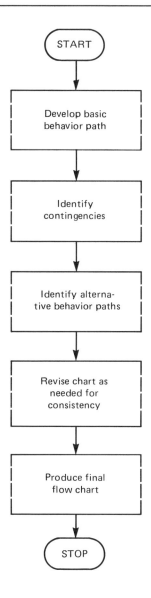

Figure 3.18. Flow Chart Technique.

3. Identify alternative behaviors which branch from each decision point. All branches must eventually loop back into the main path. Rather than write a repetition of a process, always loop back to the process in the main path. When using 3 x 5 cards it is best to use a different color for alternative branches; this keeps the branches visually distinct.

4. Examine the chart for consistency. Break processes into subprocesses if needed and insert additional decision points as required. The master performers should concentrate on one activity at a time during this review. Photographs of the posted cards can be taken to record the sequence if the cards must be taken down or moved during long-term analysis.

5. Produce a final flow chart. The following is one conventional set of symbols that can be used to format the final chart:

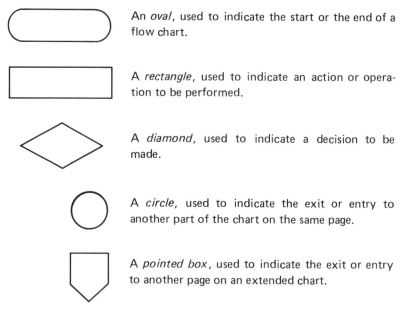

An *oval*, used to indicate the start or the end of a flow chart.

A *rectangle*, used to indicate an action or opera- tion to be performed.

A *diamond*, used to indicate a decision to be made.

A *circle*, used to indicate the exit or entry to another part of the chart on the same page.

A *pointed box*, used to indicate the exit or entry to another page on an extended chart.

An *arrow*, used to indicate the direction of flow, or sequence, from one step to another. Only one arrow should enter or leave an oval, rectangle, circle, or pointed box. One arrow should enter a diamond, but two, and only two, arrows should leave a diamond. Arrows should merge into one another rather than into one of the other shapes.

Example

The basic behavior path of a very simple task, opening a locked door, was flow-charted in Figure 3.19. This initial chart was then revised in Figure 3.20 to include two necessary decision points. The flow chart in Figure 3.20 starts with an oval. The person is then asked to perform two operations: "select a key" and "try the key in the lock." At this point a decision (diamond) is reached: "does it fit?" Two arrows leave this decision diamond. If the answer to the question "does it fit?" is no, the person is directed to "select another key." If the answer is yes, the person is directed to perform the operation "try to turn the key." At this point, another decision diamond is reached; "does it turn?" Again, two arrows leave this second decision diamond. If the decision is no, the person is directed to the top operation: "select a key." If the decision is yes, the person is directed to the operation "open the door." The final instruction is the oval "stop."

The flow chart was then examined for inconsistencies and additional subprocesses. Careful examination showed a serious deficiency. Suppose that the correct key is not found. The person could spend the rest of his or her life selecting keys that do not open a door. For this simple task, it may be too obvious to merit changing the chart. The person will simply recognize this and stop selecting keys. For many real-life procedures, however, it is essential that options be given for all contingencies. Otherwise loss of time, money, and even life can occur. A simple solution to the problems in the flow chart on opening a locked door is found in Figure 3.21. The person now has a decision point (do you wish to continue?) which allows for an occasion when the correct key is not found.

An additional task, getting a soft drink, is flow-charted in Figure 3.22. This chart shows the use of the circle and pointed box connectors. The circle is an exit or entry on a single page. The pointed box is an exit or entry from one page to another. Notice that flow charts only have one start and one stop point. Arrows are used to feed branches into the stop point.

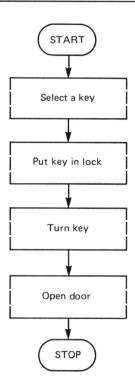

Figure 3.19. Basic Path for Opening a Locked Door.

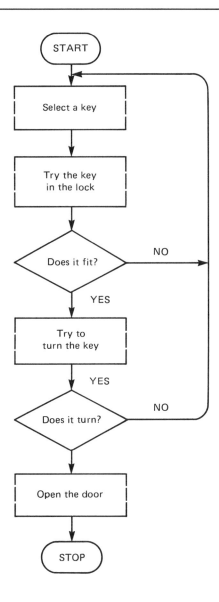

Figure 3.20. Flow Chart for Opening a Locked Door.

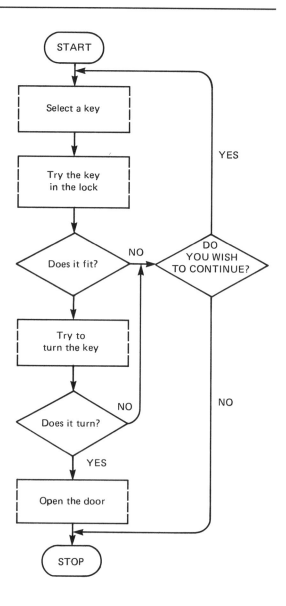

Figure 3.21. Improved Flow Chart for Opening a Locked Door.

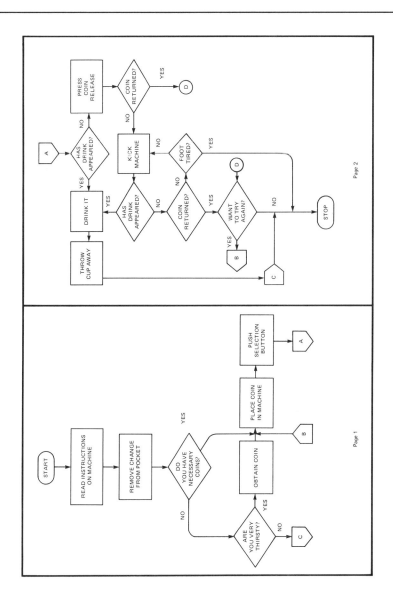

Figure 3.22. Getting a Soft Drink.

PICTURE TECHNIQUE

Purpose
The Picture Technique is used when a drawing or photograph of the task makes it easier to analyze and understand how the task is done.

Advantages
The Picture Technique makes it easy to record the worker's activities. The recorded data is easily understood and communicated to others. Once recorded, the movements can be analyzed to improve performance.

Disadvantages
Complex movements and operations are more difficult to analyze with this technique because multiple charts or flow lines become confusing. This disadvantage can be overcome by videotaping the performance.

Description
The analyst visually depicts how the task is done. This is flow-charted in Figure 3.23 and uses the following steps:
1. Decide the level of detail to be analyzed. The task could be analyzed at a general level, "Where does the worker walk during task performance?", or at a very detailed level, "What hand motions are used?"
2. Select the type of visual recording technique to be used. Sometimes tasks can be inexpensively analyzed using simple line drawings. For more detailed work, black and white photographs are useful. Complex tasks usually require videotaping. Simple line drawings or black and white photographs tend to distract the work place less than videotaping, so they are best when the task is not overly complex.
3. Observe the task and record the performance. The record usually includes an indication of movement as well as activities being performed.
4. Interview the master performer to clarify actions and movements. These can be written directly on drawings. On videotapes it is useful to have a separate audio track of the master performer's task description dubbed over the visual.
5. Produce a finished picture of the actions. The completed picture serves as a basis for improving the performer's actions. The finished analysis may also be a useful training aid. For instance, videotapes or pictures might be edited and organized into actual training materials.

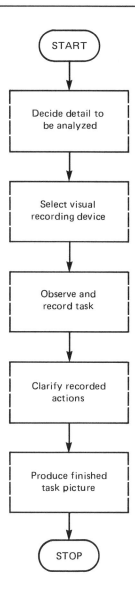

Figure 3.23. Picture Technique.

Example

   A nuclear power plant control room operator frequently moves about while operating various controls. The Picture Technique was used to analyze one operator's movements while starting the turbine. Two levels of detail were analyzed. At the general movement level, a line drawing of the control room was used. The detailed level required line drawings of the control panels. The operator's performance was observed and his movements and activities were recorded.

   Figure 3.24 shows the general movements around the control room which the operator made while starting the turbine. The Process Chart Technique symbols (see page 73) were used to classify the activities. Two operations were performed, three inspections were done, eight transportations were made totaling 58 feet, and three delays were experienced.

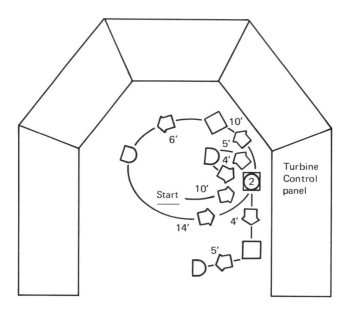

Figure 3.24. Picture of Movements to Start Turbine.

Figure 3.25 shows three detailed steps used to start the turbine. The operator first pressed the slow starting rate pushbutton (1), then pressed the 100 RPM pushbutton (2), then watched the speed increasing indication which changed to the at-set speed indication when the turbine reached 100 RPM (3).

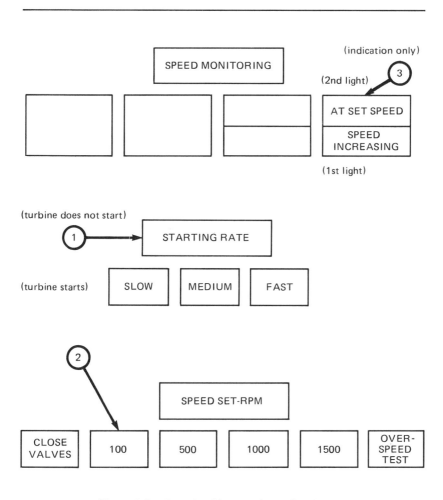

Figure 3.25. Detailed Picture of Turbine Startup.

DECISION TECHNIQUE

Purpose

The Decision Technique is used when a task is essentially nonsequential or when various decisions must be made, based upon the symptoms of a particular situation, in order to select the correct procedure. The Decision Technique is ideal for trouble-shooting and diagnostic tasks.

Advantages

The Decision Technique helps workers solve complex decisions by simplifying critical inputs to which master performers respond. It describes task elements conceptually for ease of understanding. It concisely describes tasks so information is greatly reduced. The desired sequence of decisions is shown. The finished product is a valuable job and training aid.

Disadvantages

It is easier to show sequences of action with a flow chart or list because the Decision Technique removes much of the step-by-step procedural information. Since they do not include basic procedural information and are seldom used, decision diagrams may be misunderstood and novice workers may not be able to take appropriate actions.

Description

The analyst determines the information needed to solve problems and produces a decision diagram. This process is flow-charted in Figure 3.26 and uses the following steps:

1. Define the decision that must be made or the problem that must be solved. Decisions and problems result when the task involves multiple stimuli or fine distinctions. Even simple tasks involve distinctions that could be analyzed. For example, a cook may be required to melt butter for a recipe—a seemingly simple task. Yet an important distinction may need to be made between just melted butter, boiling butter, and burned butter.

   A golfer's swing may be described in detail with one of the other techniques. It would be helpful, however, to use the Decision Technique to show the difference between swings that result in a hook, slice, or drive.

   The decision or problem is identified by asking a master performer questions like "What could cause confusion in this task?" and "What decision must be made?" The answers to these questions are then written in the form illustrated by the following statements:

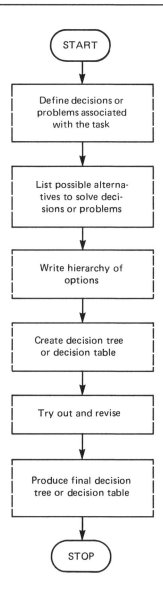

Figure 3.26. Decision Technique.

- When should the various golf swings be used?
- What should I do to fix noisy mechanical equipment?
- Which chemical test would be best for analyzing this substance?

2. List the possible alternatives (or use the alternatives generated by other analysis techniques) which solve the decision or problem. Then describe the alternatives' discriminating characteristics. For instance, the following alternatives and characteristics distinguish when to use various golf swings:

   - Drive—ball flies straight away from golfer at a reasonably low arch.
   - Hook—ball flies away from, and curves towards golfer.
   - Slice—ball flies away from, and curves away from golfer.
   - Chip—ball flies away with a very high arch for a short distance.

3. Write a hierarchy of options, based upon the discriminating characteristics, which lead to the correct or most likely identification of each alternative. Each option has at least two parts: the "if" and the "then." The master performer completes the sentence "If (*alternative*) occurs, then do (*action*)." Some decisions involve multiple criteria as illustrated by the sentence: "If (*alternative*) and if (*alternative*) and if (*alternative*) then do (*action*)." Discriminating characteristics can even be associated with possible alternatives by completing the sentence "If the following conditions exist . . . . , then (% of the time) the solution is (action)." Options might be written as follows:

If   —The infection is primarily bacteremia, and the gastrointestinal tract is the likely entry, and the sterile sites contain the culture of bacteroids.

Then   —There is .7 percent chance of bacteroids.

If   —Supervision is constantly changing, and workers have only generalized instructions, and job related feedback is poor, and no incentives for good work exist.

Then   —There is little chance (.05 percent) that technical training will change productivity.

Charting helps describe the options. Various formats of "Decision Tables" can be used, or the "Decision Tree" can be used (Figure 3.27). During initial description, the Decision Tree format often works best. Master performers can meet as a group and brainstorm "if/then" statements while the analyst writes these on cards and posts them as a decision tree on a blank wall. After the initial description, the decision tree is usually changed to the "Decision Table" format.

DECISION TABLES

If	Then
A	1
B	2
C	3

If	And If	Then
A	M	1
	N	2
	O	3
B	P	4
	Q	5
C	R	6

	And If C	And If D
If A	Then 1	Then 2
If B	Then 3	Then 4

If	And If	And If	Then
A	D	J	1
		K	2
	E	L	3
		M	4
B	F	N	5
		O	6
	G	P	7
		Q	8
C	H	R	9
	I	S	10

If	Then
A	
B	1
C	
D	
E	2

If	Then
A	1
	2
	3
B	4
	5
	6
C	7

If			
A	YES	YES	NO
B	NO	YES	NO
C	NO	NO	NO
Then			
1	X		
2		X	2
3			1

DECISION TREES

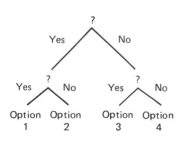

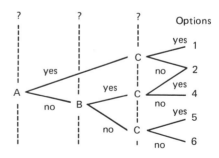

Figure 3.27. Decision Analysis Formats.

4. Create a formal decision analysis by formatting the decisions as a decision tree or decision table (Figure 3.27).
5. Test the completed analysis by having a previously uninvolved master performer try out the decisions, and revise the analysis as required.
6. Produce the final decision tree or decision table.

Example

A critical task for control room operators of a nuclear power plant is to ensure the turbine stops (trips) when the reactor stops (trips). Several decisions must be made to determine that the turbine has stopped. A master reactor operator discussed these decisions and the analyst listed the following options:

1. If the reactor trip alarm sounds, the operator checks the turbine trip indicator.
2. If the indicator is on (white), the operator checks the turbine speed gauge.
3. If speed is increasing, the operator manually trips the turbine.
4. If the speed remains steady at 1500 RPM, the operator checks the megawatt meter.
5. If the megawatt meter is greater than zero, the operator checks the generator breaker indicator.
6. If the generator breaker indicator is red, the operator manually trips the turbine and also the EHC pump.
7. If the turbine trip indicator is off, the operator depresses the turbine trip button and rechecks all previous considerations.
8. If the turbine trip indicator is on and turbine speed is decreasing and the megawatt meter is zero and the generator breaker indicator light is green and white, then the turbine has tripped.

After the initial listing, the analyst created a decision table which summarized the options. After trying the initial table, revisions were made. A portion of the final table is shown in Figure 3.28. This summarizes the decisions made by the operator.

To use the chart in Figure 3.28, the operator could enter the chart at any point and move progressively down each column, answering questions until all options match the particular situation. The correct actions for each situation are listed directly below each column of options. For instance, if the white turbine trip indicator is not on (first column), the operator (1) depresses the turbine trip button and (2) rechecks the white turbine trip indicator. If the turbine trip indicator white light is on and the turbine speed gauge is increasing (second column), then (1) the turbine is tripped manually and (2) the turbine stops. When the final column of options matches, the turbine is tripped (X).

What decisions are required to respond to a reactor trip alarm?

CONDITIONS	OPTIONS			
1. White turbine trip indicator light on	NO	YES	YES	YES
2. Turbine speed gage increasing	-	YES	NO	NO
3. Turbine speed guage steady (1500 rpm)	-	-	YES	NO
4. Mega watt meter reads zero	-	-	NO	YES
5. Generator breaker indicator light red	-	-	YES	NO
6. Generator breaker indicator light green and white	-	-	-	YES
ACTIONS	DECISIONS			
Depress turbine trip button	1			
Recheck turbine trip indicator (1 above)	2			
Manually trip turbine		1	1	
Trip EHC pump			2	
Turbine tripped (stop)		2	3	X

(- means not applicable)

Figure 3.28. Example Decision Table.

Chapter Summary

Various techniques can be used to describe how the job is done—a prerequisite to correct performance. Some techniques provide overall descriptions and task categorization. Others stress the interface of operators and machines. Still others describe tasks involving complex decisions. Although each technique can be used to add insight about how every task is done, each has a suggested application summarized in Figure 3.29.

SITUATION	SUGGESTED TECHNIQUE
An overall description of a sequential task is required.	Basic Task Description Technique
The task involves multiple people, data inputs, or decisions.	Stimulus-Response Technique
A basic description of the task is adequate to categorize important task considerations.	Process Chart Technique
The task is very detailed involving fine manipulations.	Operation Chart Technique
Time and man-machine interfaces are important to the task.	Man-Machine Time Chart Technique
The task is basically sequential with occasional decision points and alternative actions.	Flow Chart Technique
The task is visually oriented involving movements to different locations and manipulation of devices and controls.	Picture Technique
The task involves multiple decisions and concept formation or is non-sequential.	Decision Technique

Figure 3.29. Finding How the Task Is Done Techniques Summary.

Once the analyst has determined what the job is and how the job is done, it is important to analyze what the job *should* be or how the job *should* be done. This is the subject of the next chapter.

4

Finding How to
Improve the Job

The techniques in previous chapters, used to describe what the job is and how it is performed, depend heavily upon descriptions of master performer behavior. But suppose the job is arranged in a dysfunctional manner, or suppose the best performers have not fully mastered the tasks. Maybe the job could be done better. This would not be identified by simply describing the master's performance. The analyst must show how the task could be improved. This requires a different set of analysis techniques to find *what* the task *should* be and *how* it *should* be done.

Main Goal: To Identify and Solve Inadequate Task Performance

When task behavior has been described, it is then possible to identify inadequacies. Possible performance errors include poor *results* as indicated by shortfalls in task accomplishment and consumer satisfaction; little *quantity* as indicated by the amount of output; and poor *quality* as indicated by accuracy, completeness, expense, timeliness, and safety. To improve results, quantity, and quality, the task is analyzed by contrasting it against correct performance. The difference between what the task should be and what it currently is points to relationships and discrepancies which suggest possible solutions.

The techniques used to identify and solve inadequate performance vary from the creative and visionary to the systematic and deliberate. Each serves a different purpose. The techniques discussed in this chapter include the Basic Comparison Technique, the Behavior Counting Technique, the Path Analysis Technique, the Critical Incident Technique, the Problem Analysis Technique, the Performance Probe Technique, the Job Satisfaction Technique, the Matrix Technique, the Fault Tree Technique, and the Imagination Technique.

BASIC COMPARISON TECHNIQUE

Purpose
The Basic Comparison Technique contrasts the various methods of performance so that the *best* can be selected. Some form of the basic comparison technique can be used with all of the other techniques described in this chapter.

Advantages
The Basic Comparison Technique identifies and contrasts the strengths and weaknesses of alternative performance options. Since alternative outcomes are assessed, the selected option is superior to that developed by considering only one approach. The decision process is simplified because only one criterion is considered at a time.

Disadvantages
Rating criteria may be overlooked with the Basic Comparison Technique. Future performance problems may result when important criteria are not considered. Also, the criteria are usually general and fail to consider specific differences in how the job might be done.

Description
The Basic Comparison Technique is flow-charted in Figure 4.1 and uses the following steps:
1. Identify alternative methods for performing the task. The previously described techniques for finding what the task is and how the task is done provide descriptions of current methods. Additional alternative methods can be developed using the techniques discussed in this chapter.
2. Select criteria for evaluating the methods. Criteria might include results,

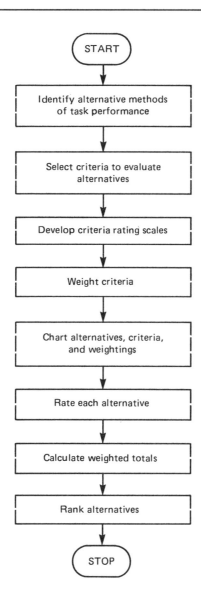

Figure 4.1. Basic Comparison Technique.

quantity, quality, cost, schedules, attitudes, etc. The other techniques in this chapter present alternative criteria.

3. Develop rating scales for the selected criteria. Each scale should have the same number of ratings. Positive and negative ratings should be on the same side of all scales. The following are example criterion scales:

COST	1	2	3	4	5
	$100.00	$500.00	$900.00	$1300.00	$1700.00

QUANTITY	1	2	3	4	5
	100 p/hr	75 p/hr	50 p/hr	25 p/hr	0 p/hr

QUALITY	1	2	3	4	5
	1 reject per 100	5 rejects per 100	10 rejects per 100	15 rejects per 100	20 rejects per 100

4. Weight the importance of each selected criteria. Typically a ten-point weighting scale (very important to not important) is used. However, if fine distinctions must be made between many alternatives, the weighting scale may have to be extended.

5. Chart the alternatives, criteria, and weights. Various charting techniques can be used. The matrix in Figure 4.2 shows one format. Other formats are used with the other techniques in this chapter.

6. Rate each alternative using each criterion. Consider only one criterion and alternative at a time.

7. Calculate weighted totals for each alternative by multiplying the rating by each weighting and adding all criteria. For instance, the weighted totals for two criteria would be calculated as follows:

Criteria Rating		Weight		Rating
3	x	5	=	15
7	x	10	=	+70
				————
				85 Total

8. Rank the alternatives from best to worst. If the rating scale is designed so the lowest numbered ratings are most positive, the lowest weighted total will be the best alternative. Conversely, if the highest numbered ratings are most positive, the highest weighted total should be ranked best.

Example

A large organization needed a well-developed training program. Five alternative development methods were considered to have some merit: using staff trainers, borrowing workers from other departments, hiring staff developers, contracting training developers, or using university interns. The following weighted criterion scales were developed to contrast the alternatives:

	1	2	3	4	5
CONTENT QUALITY (Weight=10)	Excellent Technical Quality	Good Technical Quality	Fair Technical Quality	Poor Technical Quality	Very Poor Technical Quality
INSTRUCTIONAL QUALITY (Weight=10)	1	2	3	4	5
	Task Analysis objectives, pretests, good sequence, training aids, objective tests, good materials		Textbook objectives, good sequence, good lesson materials		No objectives, disorganized, poor materials
SCHEDULED (Weight=8)	1	2	3	4	5
	High chance courses developed on schedule		Moderate chance courses developed on schedule		Little chance courses developed on schedule
COST (Weight=6)	1	2	3	4	5
	$100.00 or less	$500.00	$900.00	$1300.00	$1700.00

The alternatives and criteria were charted in Figure 4.2. Then each alternative was rated for each criterion. Finally, the ratings and weights for each alternative were multiplied and added to produce weighted totals, and the alternatives were ranked. The best alternative was hiring staff developers.

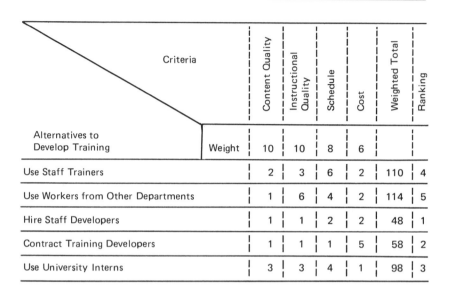

Criteria Alternatives to Develop Training	Weight	Content Quality	Instructional Quality	Schedule	Cost	Weighted Total	Ranking
		10	10	8	6		
Use Staff Trainers		2	3	6	2	110	4
Use Workers from Other Departments		1	6	4	2	114	5
Hire Staff Developers		1	1	2	2	48	1
Contract Training Developers		1	1	1	5	58	2
Use University Interns		3	3	4	1	98	3

Figure 4.2. Comparison Chart of Alternatives for Developing Training.

BEHAVIOR COUNTING TECHNIQUE

Purpose

The Behavior Counting Technique is used to determine differences between effective and ineffective performance, and to determine whether different behaviors *actually* affect performance results.

Advantages

The Behavior Counting Technique focuses upon actual behaviors which relate to poor performance rather than simply accepting solutions proposed by authorities or theories. Poor performance is described in observable, measurable terms.

Disadvantages

Because the Behavior Counting Technique stresses observable and measurable behavior, it tends to overlook problems related to faulty machinery, poorly trained workers, or unrealistic standards which are not behaviorally obvious. This technique should follow an analysis of these non-observable possibilities. Also, this technique emphasizes behaviors with large impacts and neglects behaviors with small impacts. Therefore, small performance problems tend to be overlooked.

Description

The analyst counts the occurrence of master performer behaviors and average performer behaviors to identify critical differences. This process is flow-charted in Figure 4.3 and uses the following steps:

1. Determine behavioral impacts on the job. This is done by having master performers and managers identify observable and measurable behaviors surrounding the inputs to the job, the process performed, the outputs from the job, and the requirements of the product users. The guiding principle for selecting behaviors is a positive answer to the following questions:
   - Can it be seen?
   - Can it be measured?

   If the answer to either of these questions is "no," then the behavior cannot be analyzed using the behavior counting technique. Potential input, output, and process behavior categories which might be identified include training time, training cost, injuries, equipment damage, field failures, verbal and nonverbal communication, learning time, average sale size, profit, call-to-close ratio, cost of operation, volume increase, credits-to-collection ratio, set-up time, maintenance costs, tool breakage, lives saved, down time, inventory, correctly completed forms, revenue, attendance, repeat business, amount of help, phone bill, overtime, accuracy, missed opportunity, tardiness, staff reduction, law suits, missed charges, repair costs, incorrect audits, grievances, sales-to-travel ratio, advancement, new accounts, customer complaints, absenteeism, sales, turnover, break-in time, rework, scrap-rejects, productivity, and transactions.

2. Identify performers who produce different outcomes. It is usually best to identify average or poor performers for comparison with master performers or superior performing groups. This selection can be made by having supervisors or managers rank order the performers or groups from best to worst (the Matrix Technique can be used).

   It is best to ensure that there is an important difference in actual results between master performers and average performers. If there is only a small difference between them, continuing with the Behavior Counting Tech-

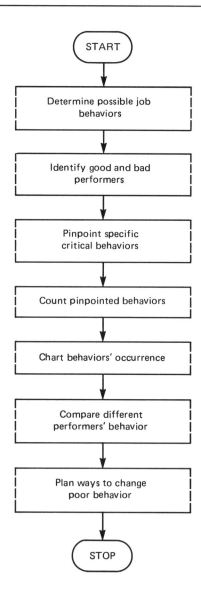

Figure 4.3. Behavior Counting Technique.

nique will prove useless since either no differences will appear, or the differences which are found will not contribute to improved performance and will mislead the analyst.

Important differences in results can be found by measuring the Potential for Improving Performance (PIP). To measure the PIP, the analyst selects one or more of the observable job related output measures identified in the first step. The output is measured for both the master performer and the average performer. Frequently the output measure can be found in weekly reports and related documents. If not, it must be observed and counted. Then the analyst compares the output of the different performers with the following formula:

$$\frac{\text{Master Performer Output}}{\text{Average Performer Output}} = \text{PIP}$$

The number which results from using the PIP formula tells how much better the master performer does. A PIP of 1.0 means there is no difference in the average performer and master performer. A PIP of 2.0 means the master performer produces twice as good an output. A PIP of 3.0 means the master performer is three times better.

With the PIP measure, it is easy to tell if there are important differences between the average performer and the master performer. A PIP of 1.2 means there is very little difference and that continuing with the Behavior Counting Technique is probably inappropriate. However, a large PIP of 2.2 shows a significant difference, so analysis should continue.

3. Pinpoint specific behaviors which might distinguish between effective and ineffective performance by observing the workers. The behaviors which were identified in steps one and two provide guidance for pinpointing, but actual observation will generate more specific and precise behaviors. Rigid premature pinpointing should be avoided. It usually takes a complete day of observation to pinpoint actual behaviors.
4. Count the pinpointed behaviors' occurrence over a specific period of time.
5. Chart the behavior per standard time for the performers who produce different outcomes. Charting can be done on a graph with the number of behaviors on the vertical axis and the units of time on the horizontal axis, or the chart can simply summarize the behaviors as in Figure 4.4.
6. Compare the charted behaviors of the good performers and the poor performers. Small differences which exist between specific behaviors do not differentiate between the good and poor performers. Large differ-

ences, however, point to behaviors which likely contribute to different performance.

7. Plan an approach for reducing the large behavioral difference between good and bad performers. Specific intervention strategies will be discussed in this chapter and in the next chapter.

Example

The job of door-to-door book salespeople was analyzed to determine critical work behaviors. Master performers first identified the measurable input, process, output, and user behaviors which were involved in the job. Figure 4.4 summarizes the identified behaviors. The figures for the number of books and the total sales of books were readily available in the company's records (see Figure 4.5), so the PIP was figured for each of these output measures to ensure there was an important difference between master performers and average performers. The resulting PIP was relatively low, but the company manager decided they were high enough to continue the analysis. The following figures show the PIP results for the average number of books sold and the total sales per week:

- Average number of books sold a week

  Master Performer $\quad \dfrac{33}{21} = 1.57$ PIP
  Average Performer

- Total average sales per week (number of books X price per book)

  Master Performer $\quad \dfrac{\$645.15}{\$481.95} = 1.33$ PIP
  Average Performer

A group of master performers and a group of average performers was selected and the specific selling behaviors of each group were observed. After several days of observation, some specific behaviors were pinpointed as possibly critical to correct performance. These behaviors were then observed and counted for one week. A comparison of the master performers' behaviors and average performers' behaviors is charted in Figure 4.5. As can be seen from this data, output is clearly better for master performers. The output is slightly different since master performers sell less expensive books more often, but there isn't a large difference in the average cost of the books sold. There is also little difference in the type of customer (in terms of income). Although master performers sell to more individuals, the percent of customers is about the same for each category.

The significant difference between salespersons is in the presentation. Two factors are evident from the data: the length of presentation and the number of attempts to sell each customer. Both the master performers and the average performers work about the same amount of time, but the master

INPUT	PROCESS	OUTPUT	USER
Number of people contacted	Number of attempts to sell per person	Number of books sold	Type of person contacted
Number of sales presentations	Quality of verbal behavior	Percent of correct paperwork	Number of orders cancelled
Number of books available	Length of sales presentation	Price of books sold	Number of customer complaints
	Type of sales presentation		Number of resales to same customer

Figure 4.4. Book Salesperson Behavior.

SALESPERSON	OUTPUT		PRESENTATION			TYPE OF CUSTOMER		
	Average Number of Books Sold	Average Price per Book	Average Number of Presentations	Average Length of Presentations	Average Sale Attempts per Person	Average Low Income	Average Middle Income	Average High Income
Master Performer	33	$19.55	67	14 min.	3.2	21	41	5
Average Performer	21	$22.98	41	23 min.	1.4	10	25	6

Figure 4.5. Book Salesperson Performance Data.

performers' shorter presentation makes it possible to make more presentations. At the same time, actual attempts to sell books are made more than twice as often in the master performers' short presentations.

Acknowledging these observations, those responsible for improving book salespersons' performance can implement the correct solution by revising and shortening the average salesperson's presentation rather than implementing unproductive solutions like stressing the sale of more expensive books to higher income customers.

PATH ANALYSIS TECHNIQUE

Purpose
The Path Analysis Technique is used to maximize the efficiency and effectiveness of a job by reducing or eliminating wasted or inappropriate activity and ensuring the smooth flow of all operations.

Advantages
The Path Analysis Technique provides a systematic way to examine how a task is accomplished. It is particularly useful for sequential tasks which can be flow-charted. All activities can be individually analyzed for their effect on performance of the entire task. Guidelines show how the workers' activities can be changed to make their efforts efficient and effective.

Disadvantages
The Path Analysis Technique stresses efficiency of the currently structured job. Little emphasis is placed upon the interaction between workers, or on alternative methods of job performance.

Description
The analyst reviews the results of various techniques used to describe how the task is done in order to determine needed performance improvements. This process is shown in Figure 4.6 and uses the following steps:
1. Describe how the task is done using one or more of the techniques found in the previous chapter. The Stimulus-Response Chart Technique, Process Chart Technique, Operation Chart Technique, Man-Machine Time Chart Technique, and Flow Chart Technique are all useful for describing the task.
2. Contrast how the task is currently done with how it should be done by determining if the guidelines in the Path Analysis Checksheet (Figure 4.7) are met satisfactorily.

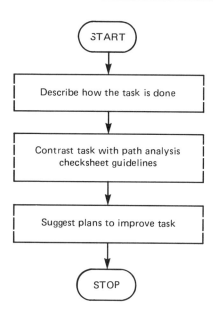

Figure 4.6. Path Analysis Technique.

3. Suggest appropriate plans for changing the task to implement the guidelines in the previous step. Revised flow charts or operation charts are usually produced to aid in communicating the proposed changes.

Example

    The control room operating procedures for a nuclear power plant were reviewed to ensure that all necessary steps were included and efficiently organized. The initial description of each task in the procedures was developed in an outline form. The analyst used the Path Analysis Checksheet (Figure 4.7) to contrast the task outline with guidelines for how it ought to be done. For example, a check of the reactor trip procedure showed that some necessary actions were missing; there were no directions for what to do when the main stop valves or control valves were not shut. Also, one decision requirement was unclear; the color of the breaker status light was not specified. These missing elements are illustrated by the exclamation marks in the flow chart in Figure 4.8. After omissions in the flow chart were revised, the flow chart was used as a job aid, and the procedure was changed to conform to the flow chart.

• *Necessity*—Each step and activity in the task should efficiently contribute to correct task accomplishment.

SAT UNSAT
    | |
—All necessary actions, operations, and inspections should be included.

SAT UNSAT
    | |
—Actions, operations, and inspections should be reduced to the minimum required number. Ask if the same result could be accomplished without each action.

SAT ·UNSAT
    | |
—Detailed motions should emphasize efficiency. For instance, hands should work together and complete actiohs at the same time; arms should move in opposite and symetrical directions; body motions should be as simple as possible and use momentum; smooth, continuous ballistic movements are better than straight line controlled movements; eye fixations should be as few and close together as possible; and the work should be arranged to permit an easy and natural movement.

• *Location*—Each task should be done in the most efficient and appropriate place. The workplace should also be well organized.

SAT UNSAT
    | |
—The work location should contribute to overall performance. Ask if the task could be improved by changing locations.

SAT UNSAT
    | |
—Transportations and movements about the workplace while performing the task should be reduced in number and distance, or eliminated if possible.

SAT UNSAT
    | |
—The workplace should be arranged to maximize performance. For instance, tools, materials, and controls should have a definite and fixed place, should be located near the point of use, and should be located to permit efficient motion; deliveries should be made near the point of use; chairs and tables should permit good posture and ease of sitting and standing; and lights should allow satisfactory visual perception.

• *Time*—Each step in the task should be done in a timely manner with the correct sequence.

SAT UNSAT
    | |
—Delays should be reduced or eliminated whenever possible and storage should only be used when necessary.

SAT UNSAT
    | |
—The sequence of actions should coordinate with all related tasks and actions.

• *Equipment*—All tools, equipment, and materials should be correct to allow efficient performance.

SAT UNSAT
    | |
—The equipment should operate in the most cost effective and efficient manner, and operate safely.

Figure 4.7. Path Analysis Checksheet.

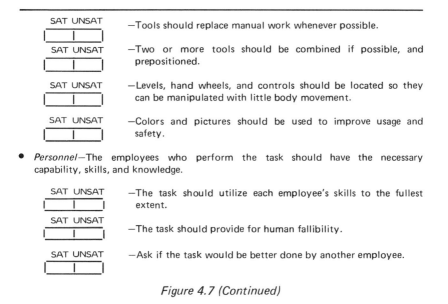

SAT UNSAT —Tools should replace manual work whenever possible.

SAT UNSAT —Two or more tools should be combined if possible, and prepositioned.

SAT UNSAT —Levels, hand wheels, and controls should be located so they can be manipulated with little body movement.

SAT UNSAT —Colors and pictures should be used to improve usage and safety.

• *Personnel*—The employees who perform the task should have the necessary capability, skills, and knowledge.

SAT UNSAT —The task should utilize each employee's skills to the fullest extent.

SAT UNSAT —The task should provide for human fallibility.

SAT UNSAT —Ask if the task would be better done by another employee.

Figure 4.7 (Continued)

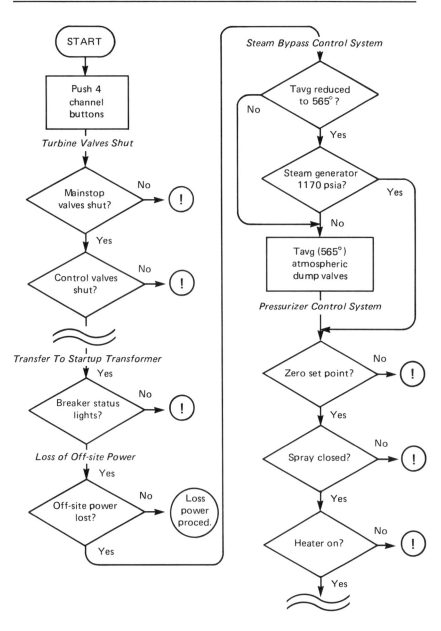

Figure 4.8. Reactor Trip Flow Chart.
(Source: Carlisle, 1984. Reprinted with permission.)

CRITICAL INCIDENT TECHNIQUE

Purpose
The Critical Incident Technique is used to identify the critical job requirements which are the difference between doing the job correctly and doing it incorrectly. The workers' actual performance is reported, compared, and classified as effective or ineffective.

Advantages
The Critical Incident Technique works best when analyzing jobs which are either very complex or allow a high degree of individuality. This is because only the essential behaviors are identified and contrasted against inappropriate behaviors. Very simple or repetitive aspects of the task are not recorded. This technique produces facts, not generalizations, which can be pinpointed as effective or ineffective. These facts are easily turned into rating scales that are very useful during training and performance appraisal.

Disadvantages
The Critical Incident Technique is not as useful for describing simple, repetitive, procedurally limiting jobs.

Description
The analyst meets with a group of master performers who describe the critical factors of job performance. This process is flow-charted in Figure 4.9 and uses the following steps:
1. Gather two groups of master performers. Introduce the method by telling them that they will try to determine what makes the difference between effective and ineffective behavior. They will be asked to describe the specific behaviors of those people who did very good work and those who did so poorly that their competence was questioned. A short group discussion can be held at this point on good and bad behaviors for the specific job.
2. Write specific job incidents and the results produced. Each incident should describe (1) circumstances surrounding the incident, (2) what exactly was done, and (3) the outcome. Emphasis should be on incidents that occurred during the past twelve months to avoid distortion of the facts due to memory loss. The master performers can be encouraged in this activity by having them list the five most important elements of the specific job and then describe when a worker carried out each element. Inci-

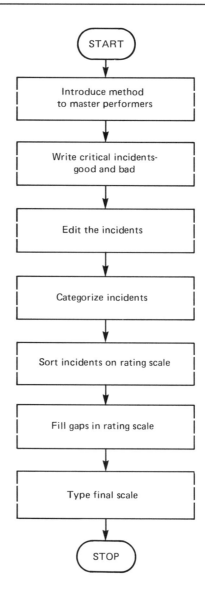

Figure 4.9. Critical Incident Technique.

```
┌─────────────────────────────────────────────────────────────────┐
│                     GOOD INCIDENT WORKSHEET                       │
│                                                                   │
│   Directions:    (1) Think of specific examples of good           │
│                  performance which you have actually observed     │
│                  relative to the task being analyzed. (2) Write   │
│                  the circumstances surrounding the good           │
│                  performance. (3) Write what was done. (4) Write  │
│                  the outcome of the performance.                  │
│                                                                   │
│   Circumstances:                                                  │
│                                                                   │
│   What was done:                                                  │
│                                                                   │
│   Outcome:                                                        │
│                                                                   │
└─────────────────────────────────────────────────────────────────┘
```

```
┌─────────────────────────────────────────────────────────────────┐
│                     POOR INCIDENT WORKSHEET                       │
│                                                                   │
│   Directions:    (1) Think of specific examples of ineffective    │
│                  performance which you have actually observed     │
│                  relative to the task being analyzed. (2) Write   │
│                  the circumstances surrounding the poor           │
│                  performance. (3) Write what was done. (4) Write  │
│                  the outcome of the performance.                  │
│                                                                   │
│   Circumstances:                                                  │
│                                                                   │
│   What was done:                                                  │
│                                                                   │
│   Outcome:                                                        │
│                                                                   │
└─────────────────────────────────────────────────────────────────┘
```

Figure 4.10. Critical Incident Worksheets.

dents can also be generated by having the master performer prove, with actual incidents, that a certain worker is very effective or ineffective. It is usually easiest, and certainly more time-efficient, to have each master performer individually write critical incidents. However, it is possible for analyst to write incidents based on interviews. About five effective and five ineffective incidents can be written in an hour. The critical incident worksheets (Figure 4.10) provide guidance while writing incidents.

3. Edit the incidents to a succinct and simple form. This is usually done by the analyst. Editing gives the incidents common wording which improves communication and the ability to compare and analyze the incidents. Type the incidents on separate cards.

4. Have each group of master performers work separately to sort the incidents into major categories of behavior.

5. Have both groups of master performers combine their categories to determine the major factors affecting the job. This comparison improves analysis validity.

6. Have the master performers work together to sort the critical incidents on a good to bad scale. A seven to nine point scale is used. It helps to tape a large scale on a table and spread the cards along the scale at appropriate locations.

7. Have the master performers add incidents to fill out any gaps in the scales, or to better illustrate extreme instances.

8. Type the final scale into a completed form like that in Figure 4.11.

Task: Correctly shut down a nuclear power plant following a station blackout accident.

(9) The operator recognized the station blackout accident, selected correct procedure, smoothly performed critical safety functions, correctly identified related safety functions, acknowledged information from other personnel, shared only pertinent information, performed all procedural steps, and cross-checked all indications.

(8) The operator performed correctly but distracted others with extra information.

(7) The operator performed correctly but failed to cross-check all indications.

(6) The operator performed correctly but failed to acknowledge some information.

(5) The operator recognized the station blackout accident, selected the correct procedure, smoothly performed the critical safety functions, and correctly identified related safety functions, but incorrectly performed some procedural steps.

(4) The operator recognized the station blackout accident, selected the correct procedure, and performed the critical safety functions, but failed to identify related safety functions, which resulted in failure to perform some procedural steps.

(3) The operator recognized the station blackout accident and selected the correct procedure, but performed the critical safety functions and steps poorly.

(2) The operator failed to recognize the station blackout accident for a significant time but eventually selected and followed the correct procedures.

(1) The operator failed to recognize the station blackout accident and never recovered.

Figure 4.11. Critical Incident Scale.

Example

Nuclear power plant operators perform a variety of tasks to ensure that the reactor is safely shut down if an accident occurs. One of the accidents that might occur is a loss of power at the power plant—a station blackout. Two groups of licensed operators were asked to write good and bad incidents which they had actually observed relative to a station blackout. The analyst edited these incidents and typed them on cards. The operators then met together and sorted the written incidents on a nine point scale, from good to bad. They then filled gaps which were not covered by written incidents. The completed scale is shown in Figure 4.11. This scale was adapted as an evaluation tool for use during accident training simulations.

PROBLEM ANALYSIS TECHNIQUE

Purpose

The Problem Analysis Technique uses description and analysis to determine the *underlying* reasons for faulty performance.

Advantages

The Problem Analysis Technique specifies errors and their cause(s). Remedies can then be determined. This method provides information which can be reformated easily as flow charts, decision tables, and related job aids.

Disadvantages

The Problem Analysis Technique does not propose correct performance categories. The solution's adequacy, therefore, depends heavily upon the judgment of the analyst. This method is not useful for restructuring the entire job, since it only examines faults within the framework of current performance. Since it only analyzes faults that are made, it is not useful for projecting the solution to potential problems.

Description

The analyst contrasts problem areas with areas of correct performance. This process is flow-charted in Figure 4.12 and uses the following steps:
1. Observe the task while it is performed, or examine an analysis of how the task is performed. Look for all performance errors that are made.
2. Name each problem to make it distinct. The name should briefly specify the correct expected performance as well as what is wrong with the workers' current performance, the equipment that is operated, or the product that is produced.

3. Describe each problem. This description should detail what is wrong, where the problem occurs, when and how often the problem occurs, and how much of the performance, equipment, or product is affected.
4. List any changes which preceded or coincided with the problem. Changes in personnel, work schedules, equipment, parts, procedures, and locations could all affect performance. Over time, changes can occur in the level of wear, lubrication, habit, and performance quality. Supervisory changes could affect attitudes and motivation.
5. Describe related tasks, conditions, workers, equipment, products, locations, and times that could be expected to have similar problems, but do not.
6. List all different or distinctive features that separate the performance problem area from the similar unaffected areas.
7. Identify the major factors which might be causing the faulty performance. These factors should explain the distinctive features previously identified.
8. Detail the most probable causes underlying each major factor. Again, the causes should explain the distinctive features of the problem.
9. Identify the evidence that has or can be collected to support each probable cause. Some evidence is easily identified and should be readily available. For instance, tears, breaks, and blemishes are immediate evidence of a worn or broken part. Other evidence is not found so easily. A case study may need to be conducted to collect evidence of some causes. In general, it is best to use the most available and immediate evidence which supports each cause.
10. Analyze the evidence and select the most probable cause of the problem. The Basic Comparison Technique or the Behavior Counting Technique can be used during this analysis to contrast the causes.
11. Propose a plan for actually solving the problem and improving performance.

Example

The word processing department at a branch office of a large company had a problem—too many errors were being made in documents sent for revision. To solve this problem the analyst interviewed those involved and filled out the Problem Analysis Job Aid (Figure 4.13). Analysis results showed that night shift turnover and poorly trained word processors were the major contributors to this problem. The proposed solution was to avoid assigning revision work to the night shift since conditions for decreasing turnover and keeping well trained employees could not be changed.

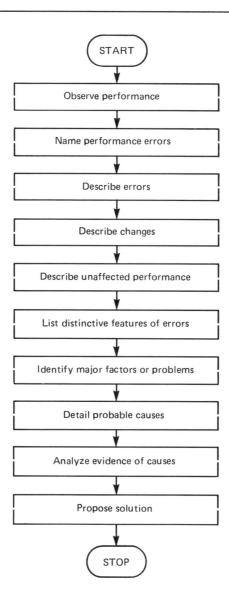

Figure 4.12. Problem Analysis Technique.

NAME PROBLEM

Expected Performance: Word Processors should correctly edit documents returned for revision.

Problem: Word Processing revision errors.

DESCRIBE PROBLEM	
What is wrong?	What similar things are not wrong?
Many documents sent to word processing for editing are revised incorrectly.	Original typing done by word processing has few errors.

Object/Event Distinctions: Revisions are incorrect more often than original typing.

Where is the problem occurring?	What similar locations do not have the problem?
At a branch office of the company located 50 miles from the town where most employees live.	Editing done at the central office is usually correct.

Location Distinctions: The problem usually occurs at a distantly located branch office.

When does the problem occur?	What similar times do not have the the problem?
The problem is worst after the night shift.	Daytime typing is usually error free.

Time Distinctions: The problem occurs only during the night shift.

What part or amount has the problem?	What similar part or amount does not have the problem?
Most errors are made when moving text around.	Few errors are made when simply correcting misspelling.

Extent Distinctions: The problem occurs when doing complex movements of text.

Figure 4.13. Problem Analysis Job Aid.

Who is involved during the problem?	What similar people are not involved during the problem?
Night shift word processors at the branch office.	Day shift word processors at the branch office and all central office word processors.

People Distinctions: Only night shift word processors at the branch office are involved during the problem.

What changes precede or coincide with the problem?	What has not changed?
Night shift word processing personnel continually turn over.	Machinery is the same. Other shifts have low personnel turnover.

Change Distinctions: Only night shift has turnover problems.

IDENTIFY PROBABLE CAUSES		
Major Factor	Causes	Verification Evidence
1. Night shift turnover	-Distant branch office -Undesirable work hours	-Interview to see why turnover is high
2. Poorly trained word processors	-Turnover reduces training time -Complex tasks more difficult to learn	-Test employees to see if they can perform complex tasks

PROPOSED SOLUTION
Since the night shift work is essential and increased pay for night shift workers is not possible, turnover at the branch office will continue. It is suggested that the night shift only be assigned original typing, which is less complex, and that all editing be assigned to dayshift word processors.

Figure 4.13 (Continued)

PERFORMANCE PROBE TECHNIQUE

Purpose
The Performance Probe Technique is used to assess the information, resource, and motivation requirements of the job and the worker in order to suggest needed improvements.

Advantages
The Performance Probe Technique quickly assesses critically important job requirements. It suggests the best sequence for addressing problems. Both environmental and behavioral aspects of the job are considered. Solutions are often simple and cost-effective.

Disadvantages
The Performance Probe Technique tends to identify real problems that management is unwilling or unable to change. It also refocuses attention from proposed solutions to problem identification which is very appropriate from the analyst's perspective, but is often very frustrating for those proposing solutions.

Description
The analyst reviews the job against correct performance categories. This process is flow-charted in Figure 4.14 and uses the following steps.
1. Describe the current situation and proposed solutions. Master performers or managers usually have an idea of performance problems and of possible solutions. It is important to solicit these ideas first for two reasons: the problems which are described provide the boundaries for the analysis, and the description shows the master performers that their inputs are receiving attention.
2. Describe the current situation with regard to each of the performance probe categories. Descriptions are developed by observing the performance and interviewing master performers. Previously completed task inventories or task descriptions and job aids give helpful input to the description. Each category, detailed in the Performance Probe Job Aid (Figure 4.15), relates to correct performance. The information category probes directions, standards, and feedback. The resource category probes tools, equipment, procedures, materials, and work conditions. The incentive category probes

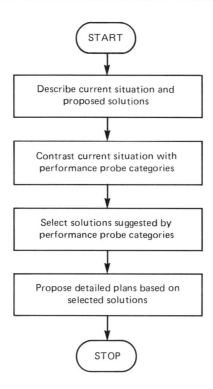

Figure 4.14. Performance Probe Technique.

salary, advancement, recognition, and appropriate rewards and conse-quences. The training category probes workers' understanding, skills, and retraining. The personnel category probes worker ability and selection. Finally, the motivation category probes worker desire.

3. Select appropriate solutions for any deficiencies described in the current situation. Basic solutions which naturally follow from each performance probe category are shown in the Performance Probe Job Aid (Figure 4.15). The solutions should be ordered with information solutions first, followed

1. *Describe the current situation and proposed solutions.* Computer services wants to hire two full-time trainers to train users of the XYZ computer system. They have been deluged by calls from users who do not understand the system or the five-volume user manual.

2. INFORMATION PROBES	DESCRIBE CURRENT SITUATION
A. Task directions are work related, sufficient, accessible, accurate, understandable, simple, up-to-date, and timely.	A. Users have no direction about computer usage from their supervisors. They are simply assigned. Each department has at least one performer who has learned to use the system on his/her own and is teaching others.
B. Task standards are clear, related to directions, measurable, and reasonable.	B. No specific standards for performance exist.
C. Feedback is related to standards, immediate, frequent, selective, and educational.	C. Some supervisors give job-related feedback about performance, but the majority of the users receive little feedback.

Solutions: Revise task directions, standards, and feedback to meet probe criteria.

PLAN BASED ON INFORMATION PROBES

Reorganize supervisory organization. One knowledgeable user from each department should be assigned to teach others and answer questions. Those assigned should use an expert contact person at computer services to answer specific questions. Supervisors should be asked to give specific feedback to employees who use the computer system.

3. RESOURCE PROBES	DESCRIBE CURRENT SITUATION
A. Tools and equipment are available, reliable, efficient, and safe.	A. There is easy access to computer terminals.
B. Procedures are appropriate to the job, efficient, and effective.	B. The procedures are very detailed and difficult to use. They are set up for computer expert use rather than job related use.
C. Materials, supplies, and assistance are available and efficient.	C. Assistance is poorly organized. One person is handling calls from all users.
D. Work conditions are comfortable and without interference.	D. Work conditions are adequate.

Figure 4.15. Example Performance Probe Job Aid.

Solutions: Provide correct tools, equipment, procedures, materials, supplies, assistance, and work conditions.

PLAN BASED ON RESOURCE PROBES

The user manuals should be reduced and revised to meet each department's needs. A specific contact person at Computer Services should be assigned to answer questions.

4. INCENTIVE PROBES	DESCRIBE CURRENT SITUATION
A. Salary, bonuses, raises, and advancement are competitive and based on performance.	A. This is fine with the exception of a few secretary users who should be advanced.
B. Recognition is given for good performance and is well scheduled.	B. Formal recognition does not exist, but users seem pleased to be selected to use the system.
C. Appropriate consequences which are well communicated, result if performance is poor.	C. The company performance audit system seems to handle consequences well.
D. Rewards and incentives for *poor* performance do not exist.	D. Negative incentives do not seem to be involved in this job.

Solutions: Provide competitive benefits, well scheduled recognition, and appropriate consequences for poor performance. Remove incentives for poor performance.

PLAN BASED ON INCENTIVE PROBES

Upgrade secretaries who are using the computer system in ways requiring technical skill.

5. TRAINING PROBES	DESCRIBE CURRENT SITUATION
A. Workers understand essential work-related theory and technical concepts.	A. Workers understand the theory needed to do their jobs.
B. Workers possess basic skills (reading, writing, analysis) and specialized skills.	B. Workers lack understanding of how to use the computer system.
C. Retraining and practice exists for critical tasks that are seldom performed.	C. Not important to this job since most users often use the system.

Figure 4.15 (Continued)

| D. Job aids are available to help performance. | D. No specific job aids exist. |
| E. Training materials are adequate, understandable, and well presented. | E. There are no training materials. |

Solutions: Provide formal training for lack of work-related theory, lack of technical concepts, and lack of basic skills. Provide formal and on-the-job training for lack of specialized skill. Provide practice for seldom performed tasks. Produce job aids and training materials.

PLAN BASED ON TRAINING PROBES

Create job aids for each department that uses the computer system. Develop computer-assisted instruction which introduces new users to the system. Do not hire full-time lecture trainers.

6. PERSONNEL PROBES	DESCRIBE CURRENT SITUATION
A. Workers are performing tasks which are appropriate for their level of expertise.	A. The levels of expertise are appropriate with the possible exception of several secretaries.
B. Workers have abilities (perception, strength, dexterity, emotion) needed to perform correctly.	B. Workers have needed abilities.

Solutions: Reassign workers who do not meet selection requirements. Hire workers with appropriate abilities.

PLAN BASED ON TRAINING PROBES

No change necessary.

7. MOTIVATION PROBES	DESCRIBE CURRENT SITUATION
A. Workers desire to perform well when they enter the job.	A. Workers desire to perform well.
B. Workers continue to desire to perform well and turnover is low.	B. Workers are frustrated with lack of guidance but still try to do a good job. Turnover seems normal.

Solutions: If improving other performance areas does not solve this problem, workers should be transferred or terminated and new workers selected from a different audience.

PLAN BASED ON MOTIVATION PROBES

No change necessary.

Figure 4.15. (Continued)

by resource solutions, incentive solutions, training solutions, personnel solutions, and motivation solutions. This ordering is very important since changes in one of the earlier categories, such as information or resources, naturally changes solutions in later categories, such as training or motivation. For instance, if new, easily run equipment is purchased, the training associated with the old, complex equipment will be reduced or even eliminated.

4. Propose detailed plans for implementing the selected solutions. The plans should incorporate the specific needs and concerns of the situation. Costly plans should be avoided whenever possible. It is usually best to brainstorm alternative plans with the master performers to ensure that the proposals are practical for the specific work environment. The plans should be kept as simple as possible.

Example

A computerized records management system was installed at a large company. Various departments within the company were expected to use the system in various ways immediately after implementation. Computer services was flooded with telephone calls from users who did not understand how to use the system or the multi-volume system description manual. Computer services requested that two full-time trainers be hired to train initial users and handle ongoing requests for help. Management asked an analyst to assess the computer system users' actual needs.

As shown in the completed Performance Probe Job Aid (Figure 4.15), the analyst first contacted individuals from computer services and wrote a brief description of their problems and perceived needs. Having determined the boundaries of the problem, the analyst interviewed a random sample of the approximately 300 users. These interviews assessed the adequacy of the current situation with regard to each of the performance probe categories. Solutions were selected, and plans were developed to meet actual needs. These plans are shown in Figure 4.15. The analysis showed that two full-time trainers were not needed to solve the actual problems. The suggested solutions reduced manpower and costs.

JOB SATISFACTION TECHNIQUE

Purpose

The Job Satisfaction Technique is used to determine how *meaningful* the job is to the workers. The job can be redesigned, based upon the analysis, to make it more satisfying.

Advantages

The Job Satisfaction Technique can easily and quickly assess the meaningfulness of a job. The categories of meaningfulness suggest job redesign strategies which, when implemented, have been shown to increase the workers' interest in their jobs. This increase in interest can directly impact productivity. This technique is concerned with changing the job to fit the workers' needs rather than changing the worker to fit the needs of a job.

Disadvantages

Results from the Job Satisfaction Technique often suggest that the workers' responsibilities be altered—sometimes drastically. This often affects the responsibilities of other workers. The redesign of jobs can therefore cause problems, and may not be easily accepted by those entrenched in an organizational pattern.

Description

The analyst surveys workers to assess the job's motivational makeup. This process is shown in Figure 4.16 and uses the following steps:

1. Determine the boundaries of the performance problem by interviewing those in charge of the job. Possible problems and solutions should be recorded. If employee discontent is suggested as a problem, this technique should be very useful.
2. Introduce the Job Satisfaction Technique to management and assess the potential for redesigning workers' responsibilities. If management is not willing to redesign responsibilities, as possibly suggested by the analysis, using this technique will prove to be non-productive and a waste of resources.
3. Assess workers' feelings about each of the job satisfaction categories. These categories (autonomy, task identity, significance, variety, personal contact, recognition, information) are detailed in the Job Satisfaction Questionnaire (Figure 4.17). It is essential for each worker to respond to the questionnaire, since it is each worker's feelings of satisfaction or dissatisfaction that make this technique meaningful.
4. Select categories with moderate to low ratings for potential job redesign. If all categories are rated moderate to high, the problem is probably not associated with motivational factors and another analysis technique should be selected.
5. Propose detailed plans for redesigning the job to solve the problems identified on the Job Satisfaction Questionnaire. The work flow, physical layout, and organizational structure can be changed. Redesigning the job

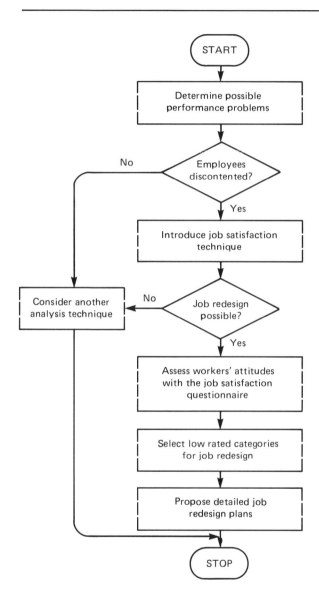

Figure 4.16. Job Satisfaction Technique.

1. *Autonomy*—To what extent are you able to independently schedule and decide how to do your job?

1	2	3	4	5	6	7
almost no freedom			much not under self-control but can make some decisions			almost complete freedom

2. *Task Identity*—To what extent does your job have a definite beginning and end to produce a visible outcome?

1	2	3	4	5	6	7
the job is only a tiny part of the overall job			the job is a moderate part of the overall job			the job involves doing complete tasks from start to finish

3. *Significance*—To what extent does your job significantly impact the work of others in the immediate organization or external environment?

1	2	3	4	5	6	7
outcomes not likely to have important effects on others			outcomes have moderate impact on others			outcomes affect people in important ways

4. *Variety*—How many different activities, needing various talents and skills, are required to do your job?

1	2	3	4	5	6	7
job is very routine			job requires a moderate amount of variety			job requires many activi- ties, talents, and skills

5. *Personal Contact*—To what extent are you required to work closely with other workers or clients.

1	2	3	4	5	6	7
job requires very little interpersonal contact			job requires moderate level of interpersonal contact			interpersonal contact is crucial to the job

Figure 4.17. Job Satisfaction Questionnaire.

6. *Recognition*—To what extent do managers, supervisors, and co-workers let you know how you are doing?

1	2	3	4	5	6	7
people almost never tell you about your performance			people sometimes evaluate your performance			your performance is constantly evaluated

7. *Information*—To what extent does the job you do give clues about how well you work?

1	2	3	4	5	6	7
you could work forever and not know how well you do			the job gives a moderate amount of information about how well you do			the job gives constant information about how well you do

Figure 4.17 (Continued)

usually requires a combined effort of management and workers. The personnel department frequently becomes involved. Whenever possible, however, redesign should be kept as simple as possible. The following basic redesign is suggested by each job satisfaction category:

- *Autonomy*—Restructure the job to permit the worker to independently schedule and decide how to do the job. Perhaps the most useful way to do this is to have supervision focus on *results* rather than specific behaviors. Many organizations feel that workers must work "hard" to earn their wages, rather than to work "smart" or "effectively." For example, one company recently focused upon having all office workers look busy, saying "keep your pencil moving," rather than measuring the usefulness of what was written. Efforts to increase efficiency by counting particular behaviors, units of time, or process details all tend to reduce some workers' feelings of job satisfaction. On the other hand, emphasizing the quality, usefulness, or importance of the final product—despite the way in which it was produced—tends to increase workers' feelings of autonomy and satisfaction.

- *Task Identity*—Restructure the job so that each worker produces a complete product and as few workers as possible are doing any given job. Some jobs are structured so that the worker only adds a small element to the completed product. Workers building radios on an assembly line might only add a single component. Trainers might be shifted from course to course without direct responsibility for improving a certain course or group of students. The company's organization might force the work to move from one manager's jurisdication to another's, rather than from one worker to another, thus pushing accountability up the organization chart. Jobs which are structured in the preceding ways tend to be less satisfying for the workers. Alternatively, satisfaction increases when a worker is assigned tasks which have an obvious beginning and end.

- *Significance*—Restructure the job so that results have a significant impact upon other workers, the organization as a whole, or the product which is produced. If workers feel that they are simply "putting in time," that their activities do not actually improve some aspect of the company, they will not derive much satisfaction from the job. On the other hand, a realization that one's activities are *important* provides a driving desire to excel.

- *Variety*—Restructure the job to require workers to do many different things, using a variety of skills and talents. When workers are required to do repetitive tasks day in and day out they usually become bored. Turnover is high in these types of jobs. If the job can be restructured for increased variety, satisfaction increases. If variety cannot be increased, then selection procedures should be used to identify workers who desire less variety, such as the handicapped or the educationally disadvantaged.

- *Personal Contact*—Restructure the job to allow close interaction between clients or workers in related jobs. Many workers find working closely with others to be the most satisfying aspect of the job. For instance, the lack of daily personal contact is a major factor which causes successful independent consultants to return to the workplace. If the job can be restructured to allow interaction with others, satisfaction frequently increases.

- *Recognition*—Restructure the job so that managers, supervisors, co-workers, or clients tell the workers how they are doing. When specific steps are used to increase evaluative feedback from others—particularly when the information is positive—satisfaction is increased. For instance, often supervisors' offices are located away from the work area. Simply moving the supervisors near the workers increases communication and the likelihood that workers will receive feedback about how they are doing. A lack of recognition for effective performance often causes the worker to seek out less productive activities to generate some form of recognition.

- *Information*—Restructure the job so that the work itself gives the workers clues about how they are doing—aside from recognition provided by supervisors or co-workers. For some jobs, mechanical devices can be used to increase job related information. Other jobs require reports on activities or results. When tied to critical features of the job, this type of information can increase satisfaction by showing the workers exactly how they are working.

Example

The manager of a large company's training department indicated that the instructors were very discontented with their positions. Salary increases had failed to improve their attitudes and the turnover rate was beginning to increase. The manager indicated that he was willing to redesign the instructors' jobs if necessary to solve the morale problem.

The analyst administered the job satisfaction questionnaire to the instructors and interviewed them to clarify their responses. The instructors rated three categories—significance, variety, and personal contact—moderate to high, indicating no need to redesign the job in these areas. The other categories—autonomy, task identity, recognition, and information—were rated moderate to low, indicating the need for job redesign.

Working with the manager, the instructors' jobs were restructured. Whereas previous practice had been to shift instructors about, leaving them with little responsibility for a particular program, the revised job assigned particular trainees and courses to each instructor. They were assigned to keep each course revised and current, and to ensure that a particular group of students reached mastery. Scheduling, which had previously been haphazardly assigned by the manager, was placed in the control of each instructor. Finally, feedback mechanisms were developed so that instructors received constant feedback from trainees, the trainees' work supervisors, other instructors, and the training manager. The results of this restructuring were improved instructor morale, decreased turnover, and improved training effectiveness.

MATRIX TECHNIQUE

Purpose

The Matrix Technique is used to ensure that tasks and task steps are appropriately sequenced. It is also useful for gaining consensus about the importance of a task and for organizing various workers' responsibilities.

Advantages

The Matrix Technique helps ensure that all important tasks or task steps are included in the job, that they are properly sequenced, and that they are correctly organized. All possible relationships which could affect the sequence of tasks are systematically considered. The existence of a relationship is determined with or without detailing the degree of interaction. Finally, consensus between the opinions of master performers can be gained with this technique.

Disadvantages

It is very time-consuming to use this technique when there are many tasks or task steps because the number of possible relationships to be examined increases as the square of the number of matrix elements, e.g., there are nine possible interaction pairs among three elements. Fortunately, all interactions need not be examined. But the large number of possible relationships can become confusing, particularly since new alternative sequences of task performance frequently emerge.

Description

The analyst lists task statements on a matrix and has master performers systematically assess relationships. This process is flow-charted in Figure 4.18 and uses the following steps:

1. Identify the important elements to be analyzed. These may be tasks, task steps, task elements, or alternative proposals about how to do the job. Many of the previously discussed analysis techniques could be used to generate these elements. The Card-Sort technique is especially appropriate since the sequence of task statements can be easily changed by reordering the cards.

2. List the identified elements on a sheet of graph paper, or assign each element a consecutive number and write the number on the sheet of graph paper. The numbers should be written in serial order along the diagonal line of squares, beginning at the top left hand corner and finishing at the bottom right hand corner of the graph paper (Figure 4.19).

3. Compare every element with every other element to determine if a relationship exists. For instance, element one is compared with element two, element one with element three, element one with element four, and so on to the last element. If a relationship is found, the corresponding square on the matrix is filled. If no relationship is found, the corresponding square is left blank. Various questions can be asked to assess different types of relationships:

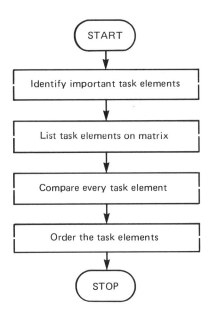

Figure 4.18. Matrix Technique.

—Is there a special type of relationship between the two elements, i.e., association versus discrimination, direct (one influences the other) versus symmetrical (both independently influence each other), or immediate (direct relationship) versus indirect (influence results through a third relationship)?

—Which is the most important element between each pair?

More than one question can be asked for each task by completing another matrix. This results in added knowledge about how the task should be done.

4. Order the elements in the most logical manner, i.e., from most important to least important, grouped with other elements that are immediately related, associated elements followed by discriminating elements. For instance, tasks with immediate relationships should be sequenced more closely than those with indirect relationships. If this is not the case in the job as currently done, then reordering is necessary. This is illustrated in Figure 4.19 between tasks two and nine. An additional task also needs to

be added in Figure 4.19 to fill a relationship gap between tasks three and four. Note that the top and bottom portions of the matrix are identical. Only one side needs to be filled. The reordered task list can be used as a rating scale for evaluating and selecting alternative performance methods. Various tasks can also be grouped on a summary matrix showing various workers' responsibilities. This will be illustrated in the example section.

Example

One important task for paleobotanists (people who study fossil plants) is to systematically collect and classify fossil plants. An analysis of this task showing how it is done is flow-charted in Figure 4.20. Each activity and decision from the flow chart was written in a logical sequence on the matrix in Figure 4.21. Every task step was then compared with every other step by asking "Is this step immediate or absolutely necessary for performing the other step?" Each immediate relationship was marked with an X in the appropriate matrix square. For instance, identifying the fossil group (step 7) was immediately necessary to putting fossils in a specific group's compartment in the collecting bag (steps 8 through 11), but putting equisetales fossils in compartment two (step 9) was not absolutely necessary to putting sphenophyllales fossils in compartment four (step 11).

Based on this assessment of relationships it was possible to determine critical tasks which require training. For instance picking up nodules (step 2) is critical to nearly every task, so it is necessary for all persons who are learning fossil collection to have this ability. Identifying the fossil group (step 7) is critical to putting fossils in the various compartments according to classification, but it is possible to collect fossils without this skill if the person can distinguish good fossils (step 6) and put the unclassified fossils in compartment five (step 12).

It is also possible to assess sequence problems from the matrix. Determining the need to continue collecting (step 14) is only immediately related to looking for likely rock nodules (step 1). This relationship reflects available time and the collector's motivation to continue. It might be better to move step 14 nearer to step 1 to show this close connection, particularly while training someone to collect fossils.

A second matrix (Figure 4.22) was developed to more concisely determine the importance of each step. This time every task was compared by asking "Which is most important to the overall task?" The number of the most important member of each pair was put in the matrix square. For instance, it was judged that looking for rock nodules (step 1) was more important than picking up nodules (step 2) so a 1 was placed in the intersecting matrix

1	X								
X	2	X	X	X	X			X	
	X	3		X	X				
	X		4	X	X			X	
	X	X	X	5	X			X	
	X	X	X	X	6	X			
					X	7	X		X
						X	8		X
	X		X	X				9	
						X	X		10

Figure 4.19. Example Matrix Relationships.

square. However determining if a nodule is right (step 3) was considered more important than looking for a rock nodule (step 1) so a 3 was placed in that matrix square. After the relative importance of each pair was judged, the number of times each step was selected was simply counted. The highest number is the most important task and the others are ranked as illustrated in the following list:

Step	Task	Number of Times Selected
6	Determine if fossil is good	13
7	Identify fossil groups	12
3	Determine if nodule is right	11
5	Split nodule with hammer	10
1	Look for likely rock nodule	9
2	Pick up nodule	8
4	Place nodule on rock	7

(Continued on Page 146)

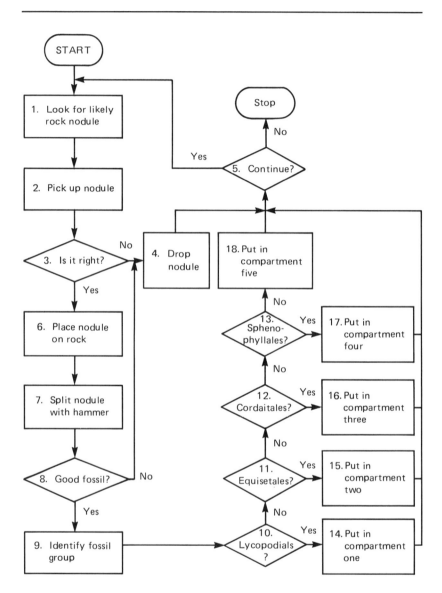

Figure 4.20. Flow Chart of Plant Fossil Collecting Task.
(Source: Carlisle, 1982. Reprinted with permission.)

Task	1	2	3	4	5	6	7	8	9	10	11	12	13	14
1. Look for likely rock nodule	1	X	X											X
2. Pick up nodule		2	X	X	X	X		X	X	X	X	X	X	
3. Determine if nodule is right			3	X	X	X							X	
4. Place good nodule on rock				4	X									
5. Split nodule with hammer					5									
6. Determine if fossil is good						6						X	X	
7. Identify fossil group							7	X	X	X	X			
8. Put Lycopodial fossils in compartment one								8						
9. Put Equisetale fossils in compartment two									9					
10. Put Cordaitale fossils in compartment three										10				
11. Put Sphenophyllae fossils in compartment four											11			
12. Put unclassified fossils in compartment five												12		
13. Drop poor nodules													13	
14. Determine need to continue collecting														14

Figure 4.21. Matrix of Immediate Relationships.

Task	1	2	3	4	5	6	7	8	9	10	11	12	13	14
1. Look for likely rock nodule	0	1	3	1	5	6	7	1	1	1	1	1	1	1
2. Pick up nodule		0	3	2	5	6	7	2	2	2	2	2	2	2
3. Determine if nodule is right			0	3	3	6	7	3	3	3	3	3	3	3
4. Place good nodule on rock				0	5	6	7	4	4	4	4	4	4	4
5. Split nodule with hammer					0	6	7	5	5	5	5	5	5	5
6. Determine if fossil is good						0	6	6	6	6	6	6	6	6
7. Identify fossil group							0	7	7	7	7	7	7	7
8. Put Lycopodial fossils in compartment one								0	8	8	8	8	8	8
9. Put Equisetale fossils in compartment two									0	9	9	9	9	9
10. Put Cordaitale fossils in compartment three										0	10	10	10	10
11. Put Sphenophyllale fossils in compartment four											0	11	11	11
12. Put unclassified fossils in compartment five												0	12	12
13. Drop poor nodules													0	13
14. Determine need to continue collecting														0

Figure 4.22. Matrix of Ranked Importance.

(Continued from Page 143)

8	Put Lycopodial fossils in compartment one	6
9	Put Equisetale fossils in compartment two	5
10	Put Cordaitale fossils in compartment three	4
11	Put Sphenophyllale fossils in compartment four	3
12	Put unclassified fossils in compartment five	2
13	Drop poor nodules	1
14	Determine need to continue collecting	0

Ranked tasks provide valuable information for selecting critical elements on which to train or evaluate trainees' learning of the task.

A final matrix (Figure 4.23) was developed to show the possible groupings

JOB POSITION Task	Fossil Finder	Fossil Classifier
1. Look for likely rock nodule	X	X
2. Pick up nodule	X	X
3. Determine if nodule is right	X	X
4. Place good nodule on rock	X	
5. Split nodule with hammer	X	
6. Determine if fossil is good		X
7. Identify fossil group		X
8. Put Lycopodial fossils in compartment one		X
9. Put Equisetale fossils in compartment two		X
10. Put Cordaitale fossils in compartment three		X
11. Put Sphenophyllale fossils in compartment four		X
12. Put unclassified fossils in compartment five		X
13. Drop poor nodules		X
14. Determine need to continue collecting	X	X

Figure 4.23. Summary Job Position Matrix.

of responsibilities necessary to systematically collect fossils. Relations and logical groupings showed that there were two possible job positions involved during fossil collection. One position, the fossil finder and splitter, is mainly concerned with the manual activity of splitting rock nodules. The second position, the fossil classifier, looks for fossils, sorts them by scientific order, and places them in the various compartments of the collecting bag.

FAULT TREE TECHNIQUE

Purpose

The Fault Tree Technique is used to find where potential causes of failure and critical faults might exist in a job or task. The analysis becomes the basis for redesigning the job to enhance the worker's chance of success.

Advantages

The Fault Tree Technique shows a graphic picture which simplifies the complex interrelationships among performance problems. Possible major weaknesses are identified. The technique also involves many members of an organization in problem solving and improves communication about problems and commitments to goals for solving problems. Finally, it is often easier to gain agreement between performers with this technique than with success oriented techniques because failure seems to be more easily recognized and agreed upon.

Disadvantages

Because the Fault Tree Technique involves specialized symbols and a style of thinking which is not commonly used, a period of learning is required to effectively use the technique, and the uninitiated may not understand the analysis results.

Description

The analyst interviews master performers to find reasons for possible failures in the job and creates a fault tree diagram which can then be analyzed to determine possible solutions. This process is flow-charted in Figure 4.24 and uses the following steps:

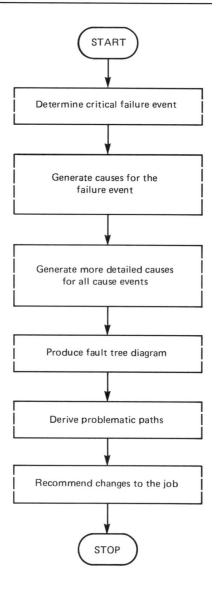

Figure 4.24. Fault Tree Technique.

1. Determine a critically important event that could cause failure of the job or task. This event might be expressed as a failure of the mission or of a single task. This event is usually identified by a manager or master performer.

2. Generate possible causes for the undesired event. This is often done by having master performers write possible causes on index cards since this facilitates creativity and rearrangement of causes. Frequently, causes are found by asking questions regarding input, processing, output, and environmental errors.

3. Generate possible causes for the errors identified in the previous steps. Index cards are helpful again. Continue to analyze the errors for each cause by proceeding downward asking the question "What could possibly cause this problem to occur?" Analysis stops when the cause for a failure requires no further development because it is a primary cause, because there is very little likelihood of occurrence, because there is a lack of needed information, or because time and financial resources run out.

4. Produce a fault tree diagram. This is done by having one or more master performers determine the relationship between the undesirable event and the possible causes. The logic gates and symbols shown in Figure 4.25 are used to produce the fault tree diagram.

5. Derive the problematic paths in the fault tree diagram. This often can be done by having master performers simply inspect the diagram to find the most likely problem events. However, it is possible to do a detailed quantitative analysis using the probability of occurrence and relative contribution of each event to the larger problem. The mathematics of this detailed analysis are beyond the scope of this book. The formulas, procedures, and computer programs necessary to complete a detailed quantitative analysis and print-out diagram are found in the Stephens (1972) reference at the end of this book.

6. Recommend changes to the job or task based upon the strategic paths. These recommendations might include reallocating resources, installing backup systems, monitoring paths with high potential for failure, redesigning subsystems, or improving communication between responsible performers. It is usually best to work closely with master performers to develop needed changes.

Example

The fossil collecting task of a paleobotanist (one who studies fossil plants) involves many steps as shown in Figure 4.21 of this chapter. A fault tree analysis of this task was conducted. The undesired event for plant fossil

SYMBOL	NAME	DESCRIPTION	EXAMPLE	INTERPRETATION
(half-circle/dome)	AND logic gate	The AND logic gate is used when two or more events or causes must co-exist or contribute for the larger problem to occur.		Event B and C must occur together before event A will result.
(crescent)	OR logic gate	The OR logic gate is used when there are two or more events or causes for a larger problem but any one alone could be the cause.		Event A will occur if either event B or event C occurs.
(square)	Rectangle	The rectangle identifies the specific event or cause of the problem. All events require additional fault tree analysis.		Event C follows event B which in turn follows event A.
(circle)	Circle	The circle symbolizes a basic event that does not require further fault tree analysis. This is also called a primary fault.		Events B and C are the primary beginning faults of event A and must occur together.
(rhombus)	Rhombus	The rhombus identifies events that are not developed further due to lack of information, resources, or criticality.		Events B and C will not be developed further, even though either one could cause A, due to lack of information.
(house/pentagon)	House	The house symbolizes an event that will normally occur, but when combined with other events, might contribute to a problem.		Event B normally occurs but could contribute to A when C is present with B.

Figure 4.25. Fault Tree Symbols.

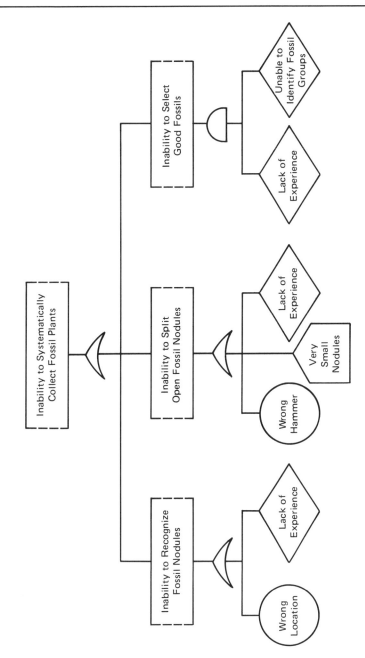

Figure 4.26. Fossil Collecting Fault Tree.

collecting was determined to be "inability to systematically collect fossil plants." Three causes were generated for this event and these causes were also analyzed. The fault tree diagram in Figure 4.26 was produced to show the relationships between the events and causes. Careful inspection showed lack of collecting experience to be of prime concern to solving this potential problem event. It was therefore recommended that job training include extensive collecting experience at various locations.

IMAGINATION TECHNIQUE

Purpose

The Imagination Technique is used to create ideal job performance descriptions which suggest innovative improvements in jobs and tasks.

Advantages

The Imagination Technique avoids focusing upon the problems in the current task by visualizing or mentally rehearsing ideal methods of task performance. The creative mind is used to help structure performance in innovative ways.

Disadvantages

Discussion during the Imagination Technique may become misdirected and unproductive. Superior-subordinate relationships may interfere with the free creation of performance alternatives.

Description

The analyst helps master performers imagine and describe alternative methods of job performance. This process is flow-charted in Figure 4.27 and uses the following steps:

1. Arrange an environment that is relaxing, pleasant, attractive, and different than that where the master performer works. Soft background music and subdued lighting help set the environment.
2. Have master performers relax. The following steps are often used to structure relaxation:
   a. Positioning—Have the master performer sit back, feet on the floor, arms at the side of the body, head slightly bowed, and eyes closed.
   b. Concentration—Have the master performer concentrate on the relaxation process and not think of daily problems or activities.
   c. Breathing—Starting with deep breaths, have the master performer

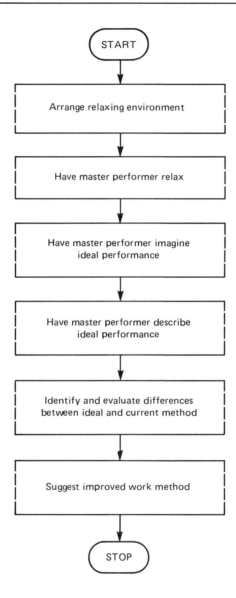

Figure 4.27. Imagination Technique.

decrease the breaths until they reach an average maintenance level—not too shallow or too deep.

d. Muscle Relaxation—Starting from the feet and moving up to legs, abdomen, chest, hands, arms, shoulders, and face, have the master performers repeatedly contract and then release their muscles. Have them try to release the muscles more after each contraction until the entire body feels heavy.

3. Have the master performers imagine what the job or task would be like if it were done in an ideal way. They should try to imagine who is doing what, when, where, and how. Visualizations should include what is seen, heard, felt, smelled, and tasted. Criticism, evaluation, and judgment about the possibility of the ideal vision should be suspended. Working from the assumption that everything is possible, they should not let anything restrain ideas. Creative formulations can be encouraged with the following suggestions:

a. Assume that any particular method is only one of many other possibilities.

b. Try a way that has never been done before.

c. Identify the dominant ideas that led to the method, then change those ideas.

d. Change the size of the task by breaking it up or combining it with other tasks.

e. Completely reverse the method by turning it around, inside out, upside down, or back to front.

f. Compare the method with an unrelated task or situation.

g. Assume the task starts or stops at a different point in the process.

h. Change the job, task, or equipment titles to suggest new approaches, or try to do without titles.

Often during this imagine step, the master performer loses relaxation and begins concentrating on everyday problems. This is avoided by not forcing the immediate creation of new ideas; rather, whenever tension increases, the master performer is encouraged to re-concentrate on relaxation or visualize something else that is pleasant like a nice, warm, summer day.

4. Release relaxation by having the master performer slowly open eyes, sit up, and breath deeply.

5. Ask the master performer to describe how the task is ideally performed. Specific details should be written down on the Imagination Technique Job Aid (Figure 4.28).

6. Identify significant differences between the imagined ideal and the current methods. These differences should be evaluated for advantages and disadvantages. Alternative approaches might be suggested by this evaluation.

TASK: Develop training at a large public utility.	
IDEAL METHOD	**CURRENT METHOD**
WORKERS: Developers, Subject Expert, Trainers, Training Supervisor	WORKERS: Trainers, Training Supervisor
WORK DESCRIPTION: Supervisor is asked to teach courses by other departments. Supervisor assigns developer to assess performance need. If training need exists, subject expert works with developer to create course. Trainer reviews course and creates needed lesson notes. Trainer presents course. Developer evaluates and revises course.	WORK DESCRIPTION: Supervisor is asked to teach courses by other departments. Trainers are assigned to develop courses. Trainers are job experts. Based on their expertise, they write lecture notes. Courses are then taught by the trainers.
ENVIRONMENT: Trainers, supervisors, and developers have their own work areas with desk, book shelves, and files. Small group meeting areas with tables and chairs are extensively used to consult with subject experts. Extensive media development areas are close to the development areas.	ENVIRONMENT: Trainers and supervisor have their own work areas with desk, book shelves, and files. They sit and write courses or consult references. Some information is shared between trainers in response to questions. Media areas exist to create transparencies and paper copies upon request.

DIFFERENCES	ADVANTAGES	DISADVANTAGES
1. Developers assess training needs.	1. Correct performance improvement technique will be applied.	1. Developer may not be accepted by other supervisors.
2. Subject expert and developer create course.	2. Learning theory applied to course while trainer is free for student counseling.	2. Trainer may not agree with or understand course.
3. Instructional media may be different.	3. Reduced dependance on lecture, training individualized.	3. Trainer may not use media.
4. Developer evaluates and revises course.	4. Evaluation and revision formalized.	4. Trainer may not feel ownership of course.

SUGGESTED WORK PLAN

Hire developers to assess performance needs, develop training with subject experts, and evaluate training courses. Have trainers prepare lesson notes, present courses, and revise courses based on evaluations.

Figure 4.28. Imagination Technique Job Aid.

7. Suggest an improved work method based upon the comparison of the imagined ideal and the current method.

Example

Figure 4.28 is a completed Imagination Technique Job Aid that shows two methods for organizing the training development effort at a large public utility. The ideal method was written using the steps of the Imagination Technique. The use of a training developer and subject experts along with traditional trainers was suggested by the ideal method. Differences between the ideal method and the current method were identified and evaluated for advantages and disadvantages. Finally, a suggested work plan was developed to improve training development.

Chapter Summary

Today's workplace demands the constant pursuit and elimination of threats to improved performance in order to ensure quality operation. Analyzing how to improve results, quantity, and quality is critical. The techniques discussed in this chapter meet this critical need through tested and organized approaches for distinguishing existing conditions from desired conditions, actual conditions from ideal conditions.

The various techniques can be used interchangeably to some extent, but their unique characteristics make it possible to suggest the most appropriate technique for a given situation. These suggestions are summarized in Figure 4.29.

Once the analyst has described what the task is, how the task is done, and how the task should be improved, a final analysis must be done to assess how the task should be acquired or learned. This is the subject of the next chapter.

SITUATION	SUGGESTED TECHNIQUE
One method of job performance must be selected from several well defined methods.	Basic Comparison Technique
The actual effects of various worker behaviors need to be examined to select improvement strategies	Behavior Counting Technique
Work flow and methods of simple sequential tasks must be made effective and efficient.	Path Analysis Technique
The critical differences between good and poor performance in complex jobs can be identified by master performers.	Critical Incident Technique
The reason for a specific performance problem needs to be identified.	Problem Analysis Technique
The basic categories of correct performance can be used to assess needed performance improvements.	Performance Probe Technique
Job redesign is necessary to improve worker satisfaction.	Job Satisfaction Technique
Consensus must be gained about the sequence or importance of the job.	Matrix Technique
Faulty performance must be anticipated to ensure it can be handled or eliminated.	Fault Tree Technique
New and creative alternative methods of job performance must be identified.	Imagination Technique

Figure 4.29. Finding How to Improve the Job Techniques Summary.

5

Finding How to Learn the Job

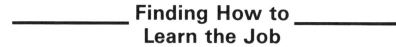

The final step in analyzing a job is to determine how to acquire or learn the tasks, skills, and knowledge associated with performance. This step is frequently neglected by those job analysts who stop short of sharing how to implement the analysis results. Responsibility is often delegated to a training department without formally linking the analysis to actual performance requirements. Because of this, decisions about how to learn the job are made without reference to the valuable data gained from the previous stages of job and task analysis.

Main Goal: To Identify Learning Requirements

The solution is to carry the process through to address the best use of the analysis. Some analysis results in documents which eliminate training. For instance, flow charts, decision tables, man-machine time charts, process charts, and other documents which come out of the analysis stage provide adequate information to learn the job with simple on-the-job training. Elaborate training courses often are unnecessary. The *analysis itself* can provide the final method for learning the job. This should be stressed by the analyst because this is something that traditional trainers often overlook in their desire to stand up and tell others how to perform.

There are, however, situations which demand formal training to improve performance. Training can help workers learn to use job aids. It can also provide job-related theory which is often the critical difference between average workers and the master performer. Training might help newly hired workers reach an adequate level of performance more quickly. Finally, simulation training might be required when it is too dangerous to learn the job in the actual work environment.

Necessary training is discovered while using techniques like risk-assessment, basic task description, and performance probe. However, the analyst should summarize the conditions necessary to training and should specify objectives, sequences, and content whenever possible. This information is specified with the techniques described in this chapter. By using these techniques, the analyst can show exactly how the beginning worker should learn the job. Each technique helps link the earlier analysis to appropriate job improvement strategies such as formal training, on-the-job training, or simple sharing of job aids.

MASTER PLAN TECHNIQUE

Purpose

The Master Plan Technique is used to tie together and summarize task statements, task descriptions, and proposed plans derived from all of the previously used analysis techniques.

Advantages

The Master Plan Technique is a summary of all previous analyses. It shows how important parts of these analyses relate. It points out measurable criteria for each critical task, as well as conditions required to perform the task. It guides implementation by those who receive the analysis.

Disadvantages

The Master Plan Technique's only disadvantages relate to the users' ability to implement the suggested conditions and measure outcomes from each task. A good Master Plan is easily understood; but, if not used, it only serves as a place-holder in a reference library. A Master Plan needs practical application and is only as good as the user's desire and ability to use it.

Description

The analyst brings together all of the data collected with the techniques used to analyze the job and determines the standards and conditions necessary to use the results. This process is flow-charted in Figure 5.1 and uses the following steps:

1. List *all responsibilities* found to be associated with the job. These are the task statements discovered while analyzing what the job was or how the job was done. The entire task inventory may be written, but sometimes only the most critical task statements are placed in the Master Plan, and the complete task inventory is included as a separate section in the final report. Other data, like time spent on the task, may also be included with the responsibilities.

2. Determine *measurable standards* for each responsibility. Standards may have been collected while describing how the task was done or how the task could be improved. If not, measures should be determined and listed. The measures must be observable and relate to important outcomes, not just arbitrary behaviors associated with the responsibility. For instance, a secretary's responsibility of "typing memos" should be measured by the number of accurately typed memos produced on schedule. Measuring the way the secretary moves his or her fingers while typing or even measuring actual typing speed, although observable, is irrelevant to actual task accomplishment, and measuring them may actually reduce correct performance. For instance, measuring only typing *speed* will quickly lead to decreased typing *accuracy*.

3. List the *conditions* necessary to correctly fulfill the responsibility. Conditions will include job aids like flow charts, decision tables, or picture charts developed while describing how the task was done. The plans for job improvement developed while analyzing how the job should be done are also included as conditions. Finally, necessary training requirements, objectives, strategies, and sequences are included as conditions. The conditions tell those who will use the Master Plan exactly what must be provided for the performer in order to learn and to do the task.

4. Compile the *final analysis report*. The final report includes the Master Plan, as well as sections describing the analysis techniques used, the master performers, and the actual detailed data. The final report will be described in more detail in the last chapter.

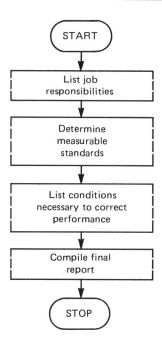

Figure 5.1. Master Plan Technique.

Example

The job of a front desk clerk at a hotel was analyzed to determine all responsibilities. Standards for each responsibility were identified. Then conditions necessary to meet the standards were developed.

The responsibilities, standards, and conditions were then combined to form a Master Plan for the job. A shortened and simplified version of the Master Plan is shown in Figure 5.2. This Master Plan, which was a major part of the final analysis report, was then used to organize performance and measure effectiveness.

RESPONSIBILITY	STANDARDS	CONDITIONS
Answer hotel switchboard	Call answered in 15 seconds. No call on hold more than 30 seconds. Guest satisfied with service.	Guest roster and message pads needed. Develop job aid of script to say.
Check in a guest	Guest reports fast and friendly service. Reservation form correctly filled out with accurate information.	Registration form, folio, cash register, and room key needed. Develop job aid of steps and script to say.
Check out a guest	Guest reports fast and friendly service. All charges correctly posted. Correct amount of money received.	Folio, credit card voucher, cash register needed. Develop job aid of steps and script to say.
Handle guest mail	All mail time-stamped and handled according to procedure.	Time stamp needed. Develop procedure for handling different types of mail.
Make wake-up calls	All calls given on time.	Telephone, wake-up sheet, and time clock needed. Develop script of what to say.
Provide community information	Guest reports satisfactory service.	Provide community information packet.
Take telephone message	Message page correctly filled out. Guest contacted about message.	Guest roster and message pad needed. Develop script of what to say.

Figure 5.2. Hotel Clerk Master Plan.

GUIDED TRAINING AID TECHNIQUE

Purpose
The GUIDED Training Aid Technique is used to format the analysis results into a job aid which guides both job performance and on-the-job training.

Advantages
The GUIDED Training Aid Technique has three advantages: (1) it formats the analysis results as a job aid which the employee can use while working to improve job performance; (2) it guides how the job aid is presented during on-the-job training; and (3) it provides a simple memory device to help on-the-job trainers remember presentation requirements.

Disadvantages
The GUIDED Training Aid Technique might be overused. If it is only necessary to give the analysis results to the worker to achieve improved performance, it is unnecessary to follow all steps in this technique.

Description
The analyst formats the analysis results to match the GUIDED Training process. Each letter in the word *guided* in this process refers to a step in correct on-the-job training: Get training ready, Unveil the task, Illustrate the task, Direct practice, Explore questions, and Document training. The formatting of GUIDED Training aids to match this process uses the following steps:

1. List the task's title at the top of the page. The title is a task statement, from the task inventory, i.e., calculating load limits, filling out work orders, or cleaning guest rooms.
2. List those things that must be prepared or used to perform the task. This is the "Get training ready" step. The list would include all equipment, tools, and materials needed to do the task, as well as required on-the-job training materials.
3. List the reasons for task performance including benefits for the employee, the company, and the customer. This information is used when initially "Unveiling" the task to the employee to increase meaningfulness and employee motivation.
4. List all task steps, discriminations, procedures, etc., needed to perform the task. This should be an actual job aid that the employee uses during task performance. The results obtained with previous analysis techniques fit

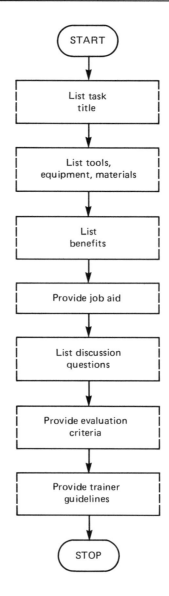

Figure 5.3. GUIDED Training Aid Technique.

TAKING A TELEPHONE MESSAGE

BENEFITS OF THE TASK: Reinforces guest's confidence in professionalism of hotel staff; provides competent control center for all matters relating to hotel information; enables employee to channel all inquiries in an efficient manner.

TOOLS, EQUIPMENT AND MATERIALS: Switchboard, guest roster, message pads, collect call charge pad

G	Get training ready
U	Unveil task steps
I	Illustrate task
D	Direct practice
E	Explore questions
D	Document training

STEPS

☐ 1. When unable to connect caller with guest, tell caller guest is not answering

☐ 2. Offer to take a message for guest.

☐ 3. Fill out phone message pad in duplicate
    ☐ Write guest's name
    ☐ Write caller's name
    ☐ Ask spelling of caller's name if necessary
    ☐ Write caller's telephone number
    ☐ Write caller's message

☐ 4. Read message back to caller.
    ☐ Thank and reassure caller that guest will receive message

☐ 5. Write time and date the call was received on message pad.

☐ 6. Turn guest's telephone light on.

☐ 7. Place message in guest's box.

PICTURES/SCRIPT

1. "I'm sorry there is no one answering that line."

2. "Do you wish to leave your name and number?"

4. "Mr. Caller, your message is for Mr. Guest. Your phone number is _____. You would like the guest to call you as soon as possible regarding dinner plans for this evening. I'll be sure that Mr. Guest gets this message. Thank you for calling. Have a pleasant day."

DISCUSSION QUESTIONS

1. What if caller acts confused about whom he is calling and asks to have spelling of different names?

2. What if guest has left message for caller?

3. What if there are no message pads available?

RECOMMENDATIONS FROM TRAINER

1.

2.

3.

Employee Performance (circle one)	More Practice Needed On The Following Steps
Excellent	
Satisfactory	
Unsatisfactory	

Figure 5.4. GUIDED Training Aid.

directly into this area. For instance, a list of task steps, a flow chart, a picture chart, or a decision table might be included. The on-the-job trainer uses this job aid section to "Illustrate" the task to the employee through demonstration. Then the on-the-job trainer "Directs" the employee as he or she practices the task using the job aid.

5. List questions regarding problem areas and alternative procedures associated with correct task performance. For instance, questions might ask "What do you do if the equipment breaks down?"; "When should you help other employees?"; or "What other procedures should be followed?" The on-the-job trainer and the worker "Explore" these questions to ensure the worker is prepared to handle job-specific problems that might occur, but are not covered in the job aid.

6. Provide evaluation criteria so the on-the-job trainer can "Document" the worker's ability to use the job aid correctly while performing. This might include a checklist of required steps, an evaluation summary, and a signature block.

7. Provide directions so the on-the-job trainer knows how to use the GUIDED Training Aid to Get training ready, Unveil the task, Illustrate the task, Direct practice, Explore questions, and Document training.

Example

One of the requirements (Figure 5.2) for ensuring that hotel front desk clerks are able to handle telephone-related tasks is to develop a job aid showing how to take a telephone message. The analyst met this requirement by developing the GUIDED Training Aid shown in Figure 5.4. The title is the task statement "Taking a Telephone Message." This is followed by a list of benefits associated with correct performance; a list of equipment and materials needed to perform the task; a job aid with steps, pictures, and a script associated with the task; a list of problematic questions which might arise during performance; and a section designed to evaluate and document the learner's ability to take messages correctly. The GUIDED Training Aid is designed to help a front desk supervisor provide correct on-the-job training for the learner by following the steps printed at the top of the training aid to Get training ready, Unveil the task, Illustrate the task, Direct practice, Explore questions, and Document training.

LEARNING OBJECTIVE TECHNIQUE

Purpose

The Learning Objective Technique is used to define the knowledge or skills needed to perform tasks identified on the master plan, the conditions under which performance must occur, and the standards necessary for correct performance.

Advantages

The Learning Objective Technique provides observable and measurable criteria for correct performance. This is very useful for specifying and testing performance in areas not readily observable, such as decision-making, problem-solving, motivating workers, utilizing theory, and learning ideas. The technique is the key to training development.

Disadvantages

The Learning Objective Technique is frequently misused by novice training developers. In an effort to make objectives measurable or fit them into a classroom environment, inappropriate objectives are written. Often very measurable behaviors like list, state, and write are used, while more appropriate behaviors like evaluate, solve, or perform are neglected. The process of writing good objectives takes time. The process is therefore frequently shortened to the detriment of correct objectives.

Description

The analyst uses the results of previous analysis to write measurable learning objectives. The process is flow-charted in Figure 5.5 and uses the following steps:

1. Meet with one or more master performers to derive the skills and knowledge necessary to correct performance.
2. Set the ground rules for writing learning objectives. Master performers are usually not oriented towards specific measurable objectives. They tend to write general goals using action verbs like know, understand, or appreciate. Or they might write trainer-oriented goals like lecture on topic A, discuss topic B, or show the film covering topic C. These practices destroy effective objectives. Rather, the following rules for writing effective learning objectives should be used:
   - *Write objectives that are specific and measurable.* Good objectives include the *behavior* specifying the kind of performance required, the *conditions* imposed during the performance, and the *standards* stating how well the performer must do.
   - *Stress the most important objectives.* Remember that 80 percent of important learning results from 20 percent of the possible objectives. It is much more important to ensure mastery of the essential 20 percent than to cover all objectives and master none.

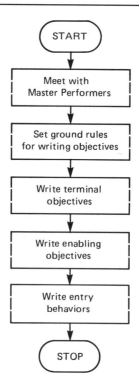

Figure 5.5. Learning Objective Technique.

- *Specify learning, not activity.* Objectives should describe what must be learned, not what will be done to learn. "Read the text on lesson development" is not a learning objective, but one way of using resources; a learning objective would be "create a lesson plan using the correct format." A good learning objective allows freedom to individualize learning activities.
- *Select the correct objective behavior.* Objectives must be written to match what must be learned even if it is not easy to measure the words that best describe the behavior. Never write objectives with inappropriate behaviors just to make them measurable.
- *Err in the direction of too little detail.* Too much detail may actually decrease the usefulness of objectives by boring or confusing the learners. Often this is not recognized by the trainer so the objectives

never improve. However, if there is *too* little detail the students will fail to understand and will question the trainer, who can then make additions.

3. Write the terminal objectives that must be met. Terminal (or end) objectives describe the main tasks the learners will actually do following training. These objectives are derived directly from previous analysis shown in the master plan. The master plan might show that one job responsibility for a hotel maid is to "clean sinks." The terminal objective would include the behavior "clean sinks" along with the conditions for cleaning sinks (using cleanser, wash rag, polish, and buffing cloth) and any necessary standards (so as to pass cleanliness inspection, in less than three minutes). The terminal learning objective is complete when it includes a measurable behavior, a specific condition for performance, and an adequate standard.

4. Write enabling objectives for each terminal objective. Terminal objectives usually relate to actual job tasks performed outside the learning situation. Constraints of time and location make them difficult to measure fully. Therefore, more easily measurable objectives are written which *enable* the trainer to teach and measure behaviors that relate to the terminal objective. Suppose the terminal objective was to "check in guests correctly" as a desk clerk at a hotel. It might be difficult or undesirable to start with this terminal objective during initial training. However, the training could be conducted to meet the following enabling objectives:

- Given all required forms and procedures, correctly describe the steps followed to check a guest into the hotel.
- Given information about an example customer, correctly fill out all check-in forms following hotel procedures.

5. Write any entry behaviors which are required to perform the terminal or enabling objectives, but which will not actually be taught. These are the prerequisite skills which must be acquired before entry into the learning situation. Prerequisite skills for a hotel desk clerk might include basic math, writing, and language skills, as well as a professional appearance.

Example

A job analysis was done for a concrete construction worker. Responsibilities identified in the master plan included preparing the site, mixing concrete, pouring a slab, finishing the slab, and curing the slab. Each of these responsibilities is a terminal objective. Figure 5.6 shows one of these terminal objectives, "mixing concrete," along with appropriate standards and conditions. Enabling objectives with standards and conditions were written so that a trainee's ability to handle proper mixing could be measured. Finally, entry behaviors for entering the learning situation were written.

TERMINAL OBJECTIVE
(from master plan)

BEHAVIOR	STANDARDS	CONDITIONS
Mix concrete	Meet all consistency and plasticity requirements. Ingredients correct within two percent. Observe all safety precautions.	Given pour area, sufficient concrete, water, and forms. Given necessary training. Must do by hand and by machine.

ENABLING OBJECTIVES

BEHAVIOR	STANDARDS	CONDITIONS
State slab mix ingredient ratio	Correct according to standard formula	Include cement, sand, and gravel. State requirements in weight per square foot. Include amount of water for proper mix.
Explain mixing process	Must match steps in standard process.	State sequence for adding ingredients for both hand and machine mixing. State safety precautions.
Estimate mix ingredient quantities	Accurate within 0.1 ton or yard for each ingredient.	Given a pour area in three dimensions, forms, and a conversion table, state results in tons and cubic yards.

ENTRY BEHAVIORS

Ability to: perform basic mathematics, recognize ingredients and equipment, perform heavy lifting.

Figure 5.6. Example Learning Objectives.

LEARNING STRATEGY TECHNIQUE

Purpose
The Learning Strategy Technique is used to ensure that learning objectives are presented with the proper teaching tactic to meet a particular learning outcome.

Advantages
The Learning Strategy Technique provides an easy method of categorizing training objectives and, more importantly, suggesting how subsequent training should be organized. Since the results of learning from the various strategies are specified, inappropriate learning can be recognized before the training is conducted so that objectives and learning strategies can be changed.

Disadvantages
The Learning Strategy Technique tends to force objectives towards very job-relevant performance. This improves learning and meaningfulness, but also tends to reduce classroom training and increase on-the-job training. Traditional trainers, therefore, often find the technique frustrating. Also, the uncommon titles of the learning strategies must be learned for novice users to understand the technique.

Description
The analyst examines training objectives to determine related teaching tactics and learning outcomes. This process is flow-charted in Figure 5.7 and uses the following steps:

1. Determine the learning strategy which matches a specific training objective. This is done by matching the training objective with its most closely related counterpart from the left half of Figure 5.8. For instance, if the training objective is "define the word widget," the most closely related objective in Figure 5.8 is "state or define what something is." This corresponds to rule one, which means that the objective uses the verbal chain learning or signal learning strategy. The chart in Figure 5.9 can also be used to determine which learning strategy matches a particular training objective. The training objective's action word is matched with the word in the chart that shows the likely learning strategy that should be used. For instance, the objective "assign tools to appropriate categories" should use the concept-learning strategy, since the action verb "assign" appears in the "concept" list.

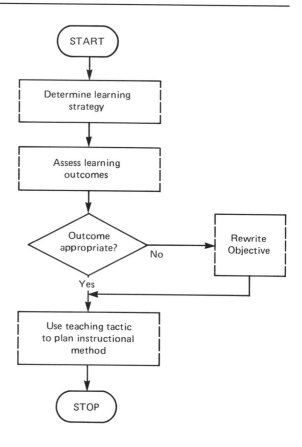

Figure 5.7. Learning Strategy Technique.

Each learning strategy is defined as follows:
- *Signal learning* is a specific response to a specific stimulus. Knowledge is gained by practicing something over and over until conscious thought is no longer required. Examples include a baby learning to open its mouth when the mother says "eat," a driver learning to automatically stop at a stop sign, or a nuclear reactor operator learning to automatically acknowledge an emergency alarm. Signal learning is also called stimulus-response learning or overlearning.
- *Verbal chain learning* is memorizing a fixed sequence of words like a poem, a definition, a list of items, or a series of numbers or letters.

RULE	LEARNING STRATEGY	LEARNING RESULT	TEACHING TACTIC
1	Verbal Chain Learning	A. Practice required B. Easily forgotten C. Little transfer to job	A. Give overview B. Memorize chain C. Practice chain
	Signal Learning	A. Extensive practice B. Resistant to forgetting C. May transfer to job D. Verbal chain learned	A. Stimulus/response B. Corrective feedback C. Practice for long time
2	Motor Chain Learning	A. Practice required B. Resistant to forgetting C. Transferred to job D. Verbal chain partially learned	A. Give overview B. Practice task C. Corrective feedback
3	Concept and Multiple-discrimination Learning	A. Practice not needed B. Resistant to forgetting (except fine discrimination) C. Transferred to job D. Verbal chain partially learned	A. Example, non-examples B. Distinctive attributes C. Present as group D. Rehearsal, feedback
4	Principle Learning	A. Practice not needed B. Resistant to forgetting C. Verbal chain partially learned D. Motivation increased	A. Test understanding of procedures and concepts B. Examine relationships C. Perform task

Select Objective Which Matches Most Closely	Rule
Follow a sequence of steps to do something (HOW)	2
State or list HOW to do something	1
Distinguish or classify WHAT something is	3
State or define WHAT something is	1
Summarize, support, or perform something based upon an understanding of relationships (WHYS) between concepts	4
State WHY something is, or should be done	1

Figure 5.8. Learning Strategy Decision Table.

SIGNAL LEARNING	MOTOR CHAIN LEARNING		VERBAL CHAIN LEARNING	MULTIPLE DISCRIMINATION LEARNING
associate	activate	open	cite	choose
give a word for	adjust	operate	copy	compare
identify	align	pick up	define	contrast
indicate	close	press	enumerate	couple
label	copy	pull	itemize	decide
match	(dis)assemble	push	letter	detect
mate	(dis)connect	remove	list	differentiate
name	draw	replace	quote	discern
repeat	duplicate	rotate	recite	distinguish
reply	grasp	set	record	divide
respond	insert	slide	reiterate	isolate
say	lift	signal	repeat	judge
specify	load	stencil	reproduce	pick
	locate	tighten	(re)state	recognize
	loosen	trace	tabulate	select
	manipulate	tune	transcribe	
	measure	turn off-on	type	
	move	twist	write	

CONCEPT	PRINCIPLE LEARNING			
allocate	accommodate	correlate	examine	plan
arrange	adapt	create	explain	predict
assign	adjust to	deduce	extrapolate	prescribe
catalogue	analyze	demonstrate	figure	program
categorize	anticipate	describe	find a way	project
characterize	apply	design	foresee	realize
classify	calculate	determine	generalize	reason
collect	calibrate	develop	illustrate	resolve
compile	check	devise	infer	schedule
file	compose	diagnose	inspect	study
grade	compute	diagram	interpolate	synthesize
group	conclude	discover	interpret	think through
index	construct	equate	invent	translate
inventory	contrive	estimate	monitor	troubleshoot
mate	convert	evaluate	organize	verify
order	coordinate			
rank	correct			
rate				
sort				

Figure 5.9. Learning Strategy Action Verbs.

- *Motor chain learning* is performing a fixed sequence of actions like riding a bicycle, driving a car, off-loading an assembly line, or using a lettering machine.
- *Multiple discrimination learning* is distinguishing one category of things, skills, or ideas from another. For example, a child learns to distinguish between various breeds of dogs, a golfer learns to distinguish between swings which produce hooks and slices, or a student learns to distinguish between latitude and longitude. Most skills involve multiple discrimination of small differences between good and excellent performance.
- *Concept learning* is generalizing or grouping things, skills, or ideas. For instance, a child learns to group various objects as toys, or an electrician learns to group both transistors and diodes as semi-conductors. Concept learning and multiple discrimination learning closely interrelate since one must group things that are related and distinguish things that are unrelated.
- *Principle learning* is an understanding of how various signals, chains, concepts, and multiple discriminations interrelate to form insights, rules, or procedures. For instance, the concepts of mass, distance, and attraction relate to form the principle of gravity. Concepts of justice, honesty, and selfishness result in the principle "Thou shalt not steal."

2. Assess the appropriateness of the learning outcomes associated with the particular strategy selected. Each learning strategy has particular learning results which are summarized in Figure 5.8. Some, like verbal chain learning and especially signal learning, require extensive practice, whereas others, like concept learning, multiple-discrimination learning, or principle learning, demand only occasional limited rehearsal. Verbal chain learning is forgotten and seldom transfers to the workplace. The other strategies tend to transfer to the workplace and are resistant to forgetting (with the exception of detailed discriminations, which are forgotten without repeated use). Training based on verbal chain learning is of little value to most jobs. This type of training focuses on "list," "state," and "define" behaviors, which are usually learned only long enough to pass the test. Therefore, if verbal behavior is essential to training outcomes, the other strategies should be used, since they result in trainees being able to describe the learned behaviors in their own words. If exact verbal chains must be learned, the signal learning strategy is most appropriate, since learning will be retained. However, since signal learning requires extensive practice over a long period of time, it is difficult to use unless the trainee is actually required to say the words over-and-over when doing the job.

3. Re-write any training objectives with inappropriate learning results.

Suppose the training objective asks students to "list the steps in starting the XYZ generator." This is a verbal chain objective. If the actual task that must be learned is to start the XYZ generator, then listing the steps is inappropriate, since it requires valuable practice time to learn, is easily forgotten, and will probably not transfer to the job, because trainees may not be able to *perform the task*, even if they can *list the steps*. The solution is to re-write the objective to match the motor chain strategy—"start the XYZ generator." Practice will still be involved, but learning will not be forgotten and will transfer directly to the workplace.

4. Plan the instructional method for each objective so that it corresponds to the correct teaching tactic for the selected learning strategy. The teaching tactics, which are summarized in Figure 5.8, are directly associated with each learning strategy in the following way:

- *Signal learning*
    A. The trainee is first given a stimulus and caused to respond immediately. If the student was to learn the name "main stop valve," the instructor might point to the valve, say the name, and ask the student to restate it.
    B. The trainee is given feedback about the adequacy of his or her response. The instructor would say "correct" or "incorrect."
    C. Constant practice is needed to establish a signal fully.

- *Verbal chain and motor chain learning*
    A. An overview of the chain is given so that the trainee understands what must be learned.
    B. The trainee memorizes the verbal chain or practices the motor chain.
    C. The trainee continues practicing or memorizing the chain with corrective feedback, until it is mastered. Mastery Behavior is not reached at once but must be shaped by successive approximation.

- *Concept or multiple discrimination learning*
    A. The stimuli must be made distinctive. Ideal examples should be developed which show the important elements of the concept. In addition, clear non-examples should be devised. Related examples, which might be confused with the ideal, can then be added.
    B. All elements should be presented at once. It is inappropriate to present examples one at a time in sequence. If the groups are too large (over eight), they should be broken into smaller clusters. All clusters should be kept in view as new clusters are added.
    C. Some rehearsal with new examples is required to ensure that correct learning has taken place.

OBJECTIVE	STRATEGY	INSTRUCTIONAL METHOD
During a field trip, given all needed equipment, collect and classify fossil plants in a systematic manner and return with examples of at least three different fossil orders.	Principle	Take trainees to old strip coal mine and have them practice systematic collection while describing important things they do. Correct deficiencies.
Without the aid of references, using actual fossils, sort fossils by order correctly at least 90 percent of the time.	Concept	Provide good examples of each fossil group. Point out distinctive features of each fossil. Allow the trainees to examine the examples as a group. Rehearse with several different examples.
Given examples of good and poor fossils, select good fossils from poor fossils at least 95 percent of the time.	Multiple Discrimination	Provide examples of good and poor fossils and point out possible distinguishing attributes of each type. Allow trainees to examine the examples as a group. Rehearse with several different sets of examples.
Given a rock hammer, split fossil nodules correctly at least 80 percent of the time.	Motor Chain	Demonstrate correct splitting technique. Allow trainees to practice splitting nodules. Correct deficiencies in their performance.
On a written test without references, define the different fossil orders correctly 80 percent of the time.	Verbal Chain	Lecture over definitions. Ask trainees to memorize definitions after class. Give quiz on definitions before final test and provide feedback.
Given examples and non-examples, identify fossil nodules correctly at least 60 percent of the time.	Signal	Have trainees go out on a daily basis for one month and collect fossil nodules.

Figure 5.10. Fossil Collection Learning Strategies.

- *Principle learning*
  A. Give an overview of the principle to be learned. Ensure that all needed concepts have already been learned.
  B. Demonstrate the relationships between the concepts and state the resulting rule.
  C. Practice difficult areas of relationship and perform a related task. This practice should be kept to a minimum to avoid boredom.

Example

The objectives required to learn systematic fossil plant collection were identified using the Learning Objective Technique. The objectives which were identified are written in the first column in Figure 5.10. These objectives were matched with learning strategies using the learning strategy decision table (Figure 5.8). The appropriateness of the learning outcomes was assessed. Then an instructional method was devised to match each appropriate teaching tactic. The instructional method is shown in the last column in Figure 5.10.

After the course was evaluated, it was found that the verbal chain objective, "On a written test without references, define the different fossil orders correctly 80 percent of the time," was inappropriate because the trainees did not use the knowledge and quickly forgot it. This should have been discovered when the appropriateness of the learning outcomes was assessed. Since it was found to be inappropriate, the verbal chain objective was removed from the course.

LEARNING HIERARCHY TECHNIQUE

Purpose

The Learning Hierarchy Technique is used to order and sequence tasks according to logical relationships. This ensures a correct learning sequence.

Advantages

The Learning Hierarchy Technique ensures that tasks are learned in a logical sequence. Complex skills are broken into prerequisite components that are sequenced to provide a training plan.

Disadvantages

The Learning Hierarchy Technique fails to consider individual differences in learning style. A logical sequence for one person may be unmotivating for another person. The need to specify a set order or sequence is therefore contested by some trainers.

Description

The analyst, with the aid of a master performer, breaks the task down into its component learning requirements to determine the correct training sequence. This process is flow-charted in Figure 5.11 and uses the following steps:

1. Write the terminal objective or task to be learned at the top of a sheet of paper. Writing the objective on a 3 x 5 card and posting it on a wall or table top is also effective and has an advantage for later reordering.

2. Answer the following question by writing enabling objectives or topics hierarchically under the terminal objective: "What should the learner already know how to do and be able to recall, when faced with the task of learning this objective, the absence of which would make it impossible to learn the objective?"

3. Ask the above question again and again, breaking each enabling objective into more detailed objectives until the most basic skill level is reached. As detailed sub-objectives are identified, structure them hierarchically. Objectives on the same level may be logically taught in any order. Lower level objectives are usually taught before those above them.

4. Create a training sequence based upon the completed learning hierarchy. There are various methods of using the hierarchy to sequence training, though the first of the following methods is usually preferred:

   - *Bottom Up*—The training is sequenced by beginning with the lowest level enabling objectives and moving up towards the more complex objectives. Objectives on the same level may be taught in any sequence. This approach is based on the assumption that learning the basic ideas first will "transfer" and make the harder ideas easier to learn.

   - *Top Down*—The subject is taught by beginning with the terminal objective and moving down towards the simpler details. This is the problem solving approach. This approach provides meaningfulness and increased motivation to learn, but increases learning time and, to some extent, trainee failure.

   - *Trainee Selection*—The trainees are allowed to select any objective which interests them in any order they wish. They are expected to eventually complete all objectives. Again, meaningfuless and motivation are increased. However, the chance of trainee failure is greatly increased with this approach so it should only be used with mature, advanced learners.

Example

The sequence for training supervisors to correct employee work behavior

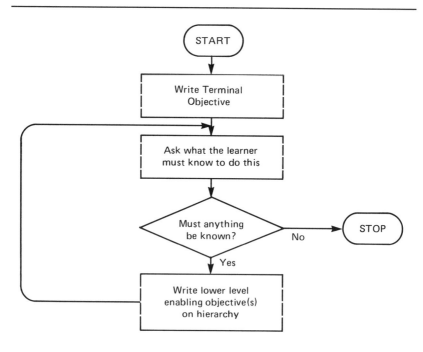

Figure 5.11. Learning Hierarchy Technique.

was examined with the Learning Hierarchy Technique. The terminal objective, "Correct employee's work behavior," was written at the top of a sheet of paper (Figure 5.12). The analyst and master performer then asked over and over what the novice supervisor should already know how to do and be able to recall to correct employee behavior. This generated a sequence of six enabling objectives—constituting the six steps in a good coaching interview—which were written under the terminal objective.

It was decided that three separate actions were necessary to help the employee recognize the results of poor work behavior: giving clear directions, providing sufficient resources, and removing negative consequences for good behavior. Since these three actions could be done in any order, they were placed on the same level of the hierarchy. To complete the hierarchy, it was decided that training was needed before giving clear directions, and that positive consequences for poor performance must be removed. Although additional lower level objectives might have been identified, it was decided

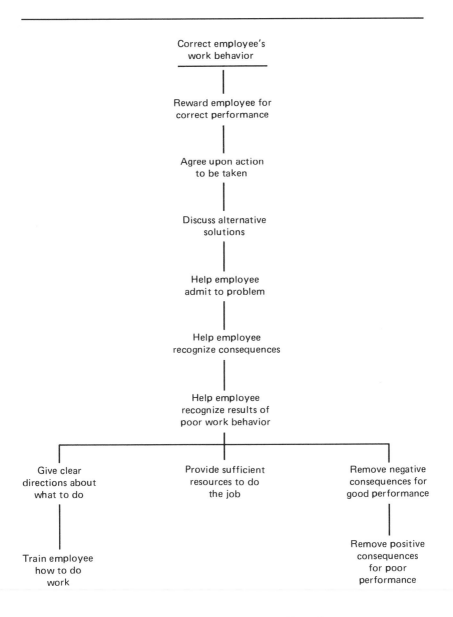

Figure 5.12. Example Learning Hierarchy.

that lower level items were entry behaviors which were unnecessary to list. The last step in the analysis was to create a learning sequence for training. The following outline shows the selected sequence. Notice that the lesson uses the "bottom up" approach.

Correcting Employee's Work Behavior

I.   Training employees
II. Giving clear directions
III. Providing sufficient resources
IV. Removing positive consequences for poor performance
V. Removing negative consequences for good performance
VI. Coaching employee
    A. Helping employee recognize results
    B. Helping employee recognize consequences
    C. Helping employee admit to problem
    D. Discussing alternative solutions
    E. Agreeing upon action to be taken
    F. Rewarding employee

PATTERN NOTE TECHNIQUE

Purpose

The Pattern Note Technique is used to select and sequence the content needed to meet terminal and enabling objectives.

Advantages

The Pattern Note Technique allows the analyst to examine alternative viewpoints, issues, and sequences before producing a final linear training presentation. Only when all the ideas which might be included are written down will decisions about viewpoint and sequences be required. The technique makes it easier to adapt the training to different audiences. Finally, pattern notes organize the key ideas on a single page so they are easier to learn.

Disadvantages

The greatest disadvantage of the Pattern Note Technique is that few people know how to use it; also, the technique tends to reduce and abbreviate topics. These two facts make it difficult for people to interpret each other's pattern notes.

Description

The analyst reviews materials on the training topic or interviews master performers and records pattern notes of key ideas and supporting details. This process is flow-charted in Figure 5.13 and uses the following steps:

1. Examine job related reading materials and/or talk with a master performer to clarify possible topics and form a perspective of the main ideas that need to be learned. Examination of the results of previous analysis techniques is helpful during this step.

2. Write the main topic in block capital letters in the center of a page of paper. Writing on a large chart pad makes it easier to see the written notes when working with master performers.

3. Write the supporting main ideas on branching lines around the main topic. In written materials, the supporting main ideas are often bold headings or italics, or are prefaced by numbers or words such as first, second, another point, in addition, etc.

4. Write important detailed topics on lines branching from the supporting main ideas. Continue this process by detailing all topics until all important ideas are recorded. If topics relate very closely, the branching lines can interlink. This ability to interlink ideas is a major advantage of this technique since important relationships can be clearly shown. The general layout of pattern notes is the main topic at the center of the page, with major issues radiating out from it, and minor issues branching from the major issues. The topics at the outer edge of the diagram are those of most specific detail and are often least important.

5. Select a detailed training sequence based upon the pattern notes and the needs of the individual audience. A novice audience would probably start with the main topic at the center of the diagram and move outwards, learning the various details. Alternatively, a very knowledgeable audience might begin with the details and work problems to generate the central ideas. In any case, the pattern notes contain sufficient information to develop various training sequences.

Example

The analyst reviewed equipment descriptions of a nuclear reactor. The main topic (reactor vessel) was written in the center of a page of paper. Then the major divisions (external shell, penetrations, and major internals) were written on radiating lines around the main topic. Important details, examples, and characteristics were then written on branches from each division. This process completed the pattern note diagram shown in Figure 5.14.

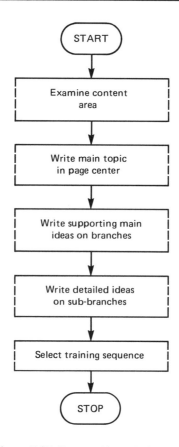

Figure 5.13. Pattern Note Technique.

Finally, the analyst organized the following sequential presentation from the pattern notes:

    I.   External shell
        A. Carbon steel
        B. Leak proof
        C. Cylindrical
   II.   Penetrations
        A. Control rods
        B. Coolant inputs and outputs
        C. Monitor instruments

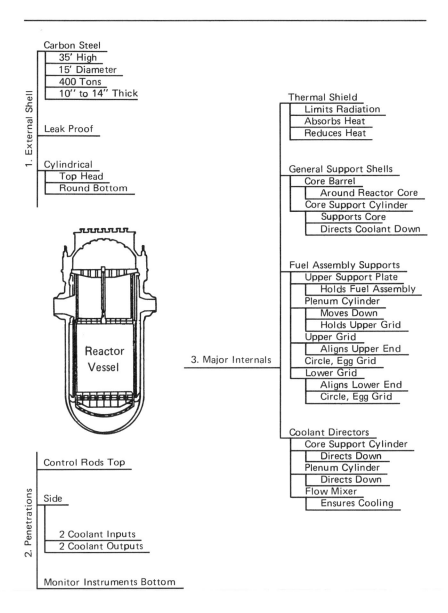

Figure 5.14. Reactor Vessel Pattern Notes.

SITUATION	SUGGESTED TECHNIQUE
Analysis results must be summarized with set standards and conditions	Master Plan Technique
Job aids must be formatted and correctly presented to workers.	GUIDED Training Aid Technique
The behaviors, conditions, and standards for learning to perform must be defined.	Learning Objective Technique
The correct teaching tactic to learn an objective must be specified.	Learning Strategy Technique
Learning objectives must be properly sequenced.	Learning Hierarchy Technique
Topics required to meet learning objectives must be selected and sequenced.	Pattern Note Technique

Figure 5.15. Finding How to Learn the Job Techniques Summary.

III.   Major internals
   A. Thermal shield
   B. General support shells
   C. Fuel assembly supports
   D. Coolant directors

Chapter Summary

The analysis is not complete until the user knows how best to learn the job. Providing information about how best to learn the job ensures that the analysis results are used to impact worker performance. Learning possibilities range from simply sharing the analysis results, through structured on-the-job training, to formal classroom training. The techniques discussed in this chapter are useful for structuring correct learning as suggested in Figure 5.15. With these techniques, the analyst can help ensure that workers learn the job correctly.

6

_____ **Completing** _____
the Analysis

As the previous chapters have demonstrated, there are many techniques for analyzing jobs and tasks. An analyst might determine what the job is, how the job is done, how the job could be improved, or how the job should be acquired or learned, using many different methods. A single method seldom provides all the data needed to analyze and improve the job, so analysts must select from a variety of techniques based upon the needs of the situation.

As analysis proceeds, techniques tend to work together to produce a final description of correct performance; however, the analyst must formally bring all the data together in a *summary report*. This report should be designed as a job aid for those responsible for implementing the analysis. This final report helps ensure that the analysis is viewed as a practical and useful tool rather than simply becoming a bulky, unused reference document in the manager's library.

This final chapter describes one complete analysis. The steps that were followed are shown, the various techniques used are described, and the sections of the final report are defined. It is important to realize that the analysis described in this chapter is an example of only one way to select analysis techniques and report the results. Had different combinations of techniques and methods been selected, the results could well have been different. This selection of techniques is the "art" of analysis; it is the glue that cements various techniques into a useful and accurate job improvement tool.

Contracting the Analysis

The Training Manager of a large training department was concerned about the activities of the Training Support Specialists responsible for providing training materials and equipment, scheduling courses, filing and maintaining training records, providing typing support, and other related duties.

Originally, one person did this job. However, as the training effort expanded over a period of three years, additional training support specialists were added and some original specialists moved into other jobs, taking some of the responsibilities with them. The job tasks became very fragmented. The manager, therefore, asked an analyst to determine how the Training Support activities could be improved.

The contract in Figure 6.1 was developed following a meeting with the Training Manager. The following four objectives were found to be essential to meeting the overall goal of determining the job responsibilities and functional relationships between the possible training support positions:

1. Identify the specific tasks performed by the Training Support specialists.
2. Organize and assign tasks so they are as motivating as possible for the workers.
3. Specify career paths to provide promotion potential.
4. Determine information and learning requirements for the positions so workers can systematically develop skills necessary to work interchangeably and prepare for advancement.

It was determined that the objectives could be met through the use of various techniques. The Card-Sort Technique was selected because position descriptions existed from which task statements could be drawn and revised by master performers. The Walk and Talk Technique was selected to help the master performers

OVERVIEW
This contract outlines the proposed analysis of Training Support Specialist positions at the XYZ Company Training Department.

PERSONNEL
Supervisor   -Stan Smith
Analyst   -Ken Carlisle
Master Performers   -John Peter, Donna Irish, Rhonda Jones, Carla Fisher.

GOAL
To determine the job responsibilities and functional relationships of the training support positions.

OBJECTIVES
1. To identify the specific tasks performed by the training support specialists.
2. To organize and assign tasks so they are as motivating as possible for workers.
3. To specify career paths to provide promotion potential.
4. To determine information and learning requirements for the positions so the workers can systematically develop skills necessary to work interchangeably and prepare for advancement.

METHODS
1. Use the Card-Sort Technique, the Walk and Talk Technique, and the Job Function Technique to analyze the duties and tasks in written position descriptions and interviews with master performers.
2. Use the Basic Task Description Technique to determine the time and learning requirements associated with each task.
3. Use the Job Satisfaction Technique to maximize job autonomy, identity, significance, variety, personal contact, recognition, and information.
4. Use the Matrix Technique of task analysis to order the tasks for commonality and amount of time required.
5. Use the Objective Technique of task analysis to determine learning requirements for each position.
6. Use the Master Plan Technique of task analysis to organize the tasks and objectives into specific career paths.

RESOURCES
1. Position descriptions for each position must be made available.
2. Time must be allowed for interviews with master performers.

MANAGEMENT
The supervisor will assess the progress of the analysis weekly and provide assistance in scheduling master performer interviews if needed. The supervisor will also be required to act as a master performer during task reorganization and career path development.

PRODUCTS
A final report will be provided which includes position descriptions and a master plan to guide training and promotion.

Figure 6.1. Training Support Specialist Analysis Contract.

EVALUATION

The supervisor will assess the adequacy of each step in the analysis and will evaluate the final product before project completion.

RENEGOTIATION

Any portion of this contract may be revised at any time by mutual consent of the supervisor and the analyst.

CONTRACT AGREEMENT

_____   _____
Supervisor Signature   Date

_____   _____
Analyst Signature   Date

Figure 6.1 (Continued)

describe their various duties. The Job Function Technique was selected to ensure identification of important tasks. The Basic Task Description Technique was selected to broaden the task statements to include time spent and learning required. The Matrix Technique was selected to examine relationships between tasks and sort tasks by position. The Job Satisfaction Technique was selected to ensure the tasks were organized with autonomy, task identity, significance, variety, personal contact, recognition, and information. The Master Plan Technique was selected to organize the decisions made with other techniques. Finally, the Objective Technique was used to specify training requirements.

The master performers were selected from those who were currently performing the job, and also from those who had done the job but had moved to more advanced positions. The Training Manager selected the master performers from his experience since there were too few performers to adequately measure the potential for improving performance (PIP) between the various workers.

Finding What the Tasks Were

The process of determining what tasks were done by the training support specialists began with the Card-Sort Technique. Task statements from the position descriptions were written on 3 x 5 cards. Then the master performers listed, on 3 x 5 cards, other tasks they actually did while working.

During this process the master performers went to the work place to be reminded of their responsibilities (Walk and Talk Technique). Finally, possible job functions were reviewed to ensure that all performance categories were covered (Job Function Technique). Then the master performers placed the task cards in logical groupings. This process resulted in an initial task inventory, a portion of which is shown in Figure 6.2.

Finding How the Tasks Were Done

A conscious choice was made against using a variety of techniques to detail how the tasks were done. The Training Manager felt there was too little time, and also wanted to let the

---

TASKS
1. Direct the efforts of personnel assigned to support training activities.
2. Organize the work activities of training support personnel by developing procedures, instructions, and job aids.
3. Advise training supervisors on procedures and changes to procedures which need implementation.
4. Plan alternative approaches which improve training support.
5. Schedule facilities for classes, meetings, and presentations.
6. Schedule audio-visual equipment for individual and group use.
7. Schedule transportation (team bus, car).
8. Schedule audio-visual courseware (films, videotapes, slides, transparencies).

Figure 6.2. Initial Task Inventory for Training Support Position.

---

master performers create their own job aids after several months of task performance.

The task inventory was therefore only slightly broadened using the Basic Task Description Technique. Master Performers reviewed the task inventory and expanded the information by determining the average number of hours spent each week on each task, as well as any learning or information requirements. Figure 6.3 shows a portion of the analysis instrument that was administered to determine time and learning requirements.

Finding How the Tasks Should Be Done

The Matrix Technique was used to examine the relationship between tasks. The tasks were listed on a sheet of graph paper. Each task was compared and recorded under logical groupings

TRAINING SUPPORT TASK ANALYSIS

Name .... Date ....

Directions: Please examine each task statement and change the wording if it could be expanded or made more understandable. Then estimate the average number of hours required a week to do each task. Some tasks may require more than 40 hours a week if they are done by more than one person. Finally, list any training which would be required before the average newly-hired worker could do the task. You may not be able to estimate the hours and training for a task with which you are not familiar. If so, leave it blank.

Task Statement	Average Hours per week	*Special Training Required*
1. Direct the efforts of Personnel assigned to support training activities.		
2. Organize the work activities of training support personnel by developing procedures, instructions, and job aids.		
3. Advise training supervisors on procedures and changes to procedures which need implementation.		
4. Plan alternative approaches which improve training support.		

Figure 6.3. Basic Task Description Instrument.

according to how similar they were and how much time was required for each task. The groupings were assigned job titles—Training Support Specialist Senior (Scheduling and Records); Training Support Specialist Intermediate (Scheduling, Training Support, Sections, and Records); and Training Support Specialist Beginning (Scheduling, Training Support, Sections, and Records). Finally, the relationships between each position were specified on a summary matrix, a portion of which is shown in Figure 6.4.

An interesting finding was made with the Matrix Technique. It was found that one group of tasks dealing with scheduling and communication had been totally neglected. Adding these tasks to one of the positions greatly improved the entire performance of all positions.

From the training support specialist matrix, task inventories were written for each likely Training Support Specialist position. The Job Satisfaction Questionnaire was then administered to assess the master performers' perception of the autonomy, task identity, significance, variety, personal contact, recognition, and information provided by each proposed position. As is shown in Figure 6.5, each senior and intermediate position received high satisfaction ratings. The beginning level positions naturally received lower ratings, so it was suggested that these positions be used to train newly hired workers, and that advancement into one of the more satisfying jobs be automatic as workers learned the necessary skills. A suggestion that the worker be moved between the various positions on a regular basis to increase variety was rejected because task identity was reduced. However, cross training was found to be important to allow worker substitution during illness. In general, the Job Satisfaction Technique supported the way the duties had been organized by the other analysis techniques.

Finding How to Acquire the Tasks

The Master Plan Technique was used to combine the data from all techniques in a summary. The master plan for each job position included the task inventory, the percent of time allotted to each task, the standards of task performance, and the conditions necessary to good performance (i.e., job aids, feedback, and training). Figure 6.6 is the master plan for the intermediate

(text continued on page 199)

AVERAGE HOURS A WEEK

	A	B	C	D	E	F	G	H	I	J
55. Type various documents (including reports, memos, exams, exam banks, handouts, transparency masters, and audiovisual scripts) using electric typewriters, memorywriters, lettering machines, and word processing computers.	2.6	6	27.5	10	28	10	27	2	2	.5
56. Distribute reports, training department instructions, and miscellaneous documents to various individuals.				1	.5	1	.5			
57. Maintain copies of training department forms.				1	.5	1	.5			
58. File/retrieve information from supervisor's personal files.				1	.5	1	.5			
59. Take minutes at meetings.										
60. Answer telephone to take messages, furnish information, and obtain information.	2	2.5	.5	2	.5	3	1	2		
Total Hours Weekly	35.5	36	35	36.5	36	35	35	36.5	36.5	36

Key:
A = Training Support Specialist (TSS) Senior Scheduling
B = TSS Intermediate Scheduling
C = TSS Beginning Scheduling
D = TSS Intermediate Training Support
E = TSS Beginning Training Support
F = TSS Intermediate Sections
G = TSS Beginning Sections
H = TSS Senior Records
I = TSS Intermediate Records
J = TSS Beginning Records

Figure 6.4. Training Support Specialist (TSS) Matrix.

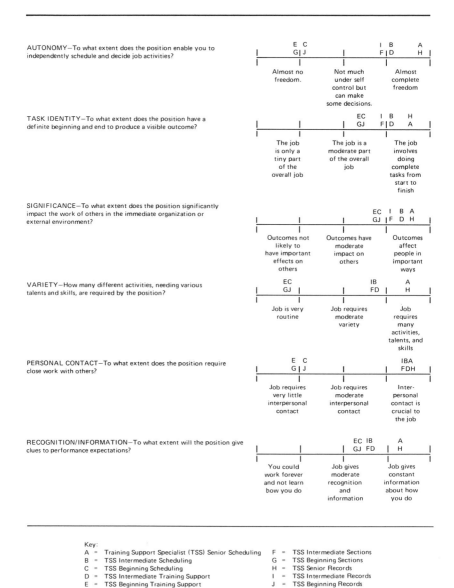

Figure 6.5. Summary Job Satisfaction Questionnaire.

TRAINING SUPPORT SPECIALIST (SCHEDULING) INTERMEDIATE AND BEGINNING

I.L. = Intermediate; B.L. = Beginning

RESPONSIBILITY	% OF TIME	STANDARDS	CONDITIONS
1. Schedule facilities for classes, meetings and presentations.	*I.L. 14%* *B.L. 1%*	Facilities should be scheduled with little confusion or rescheduling.	1.1 Develop scheduling log.
2. Schedule audio-visual equipment for individual and group use.	*I.L. 8%* *B.L. 1%*	Equipment should be scheduled with little confusion or rescheduling.	2.1 Develop audio-visual equipment log.
3. Schedule transportation (fire-team bus, car).	*I.L. 1%* *B.L. .5%*	Transportation should be scheduled with little confusion or rescheduling.	3.1 Develop Transportation Log. 3.2 Develop checklist for scheduling interface with transportation section.
4. Schedule audio-visual courseware (films, videotapes, slides, transparencies).	*I.L. 8%* *B.L. 1%*	Courseware should be scheduled with little confusion or rescheduling.	4.1 Develop courseware log.
5. Clean and repair audio-visual equipment.	*I.L. 6%* *B.L. 1%*	All equipment should be working properly at least 95% of the time.	5.1 Develop maintenance schedule. 5.2 Create job aid to direct cleaning and repair. 5.3 Take audio-visual equipment-repair training.
6. Send audio-visual equipment requiring major repairs to appropriate dealers.	*I.L. 1%* *B.L. .5%*	Equipment repaired in as little time as possible.	6.1 Produce job aid showing where to send various equipment and how to order repairs.
7. Type various documents (including reports, memos, exams, exam banks, handouts, transparency masters, and audio-visual scripts) using electric typewriters, memorywriters, lettering machines, and word processing computers.	*I.L. 20%* *B.L. 84.5%*	Documents will be correctly typed needing little revision.	7.1 Regularly survey those requesting typing to assess adequate performance. 7.2 Ability to type prerequisite to job. 7.3 Will require on-the-job training in use of memory writer, Kroy lettering machine, word processing computer, and exam bank.
8. Inventory and maintain audio-visual equipment.	*I.L. 1%* *B.L. .5%*	Maintained so equipment can be provided quickly.	8.1 Survey equipment requestors to assess performance. 8.2 Create inventory and storage system.
9. Inventory and maintain audio-visual courseware (films, video tapes, slides, transparencies, scripts).	*I.L. 1%* *B.L. .5%*	Maintained so courseware can be provided quickly.	9.1 Survey users to assess performance. 9.2 Create cataloging and filing system for courseware.
10. Inventory and maintain course materials (lesson plans, handouts, reference texts).	*I.L. 14%* *B.L. 1%*	Maintained so materials can be provided quickly.	10.1 Survey users to assess performance. 10.2 Create cataloging and filing system for course materials.
11. Inventory, update, and maintain reference library.	*I.L. 3%* *B.L. 12%*	Maintained so reference materials can be provided quickly.	11.1 Survey users to assess performance. 11.2 Create cataloging and filing system for reference materials.
12. Check in/out audio-visual hardware and courseware.	*I.L. 3%* *B.L. 1%*	Materials can be checked in/out quickly and easily.	12.1 Survey users to assess performance. 12.2 Create check in/out procedure.

Figure 6.6. Master Plan.

RESPONSIBILITY	% OF TIME STANDARDS		CONDITIONS	
13. Check in/out course materials.	*I.L. 3%* *B.L. 1%*	Materials can be quickly and easily checked in/out.	13.1	Survey users to assess performance.
			13.2	Create check in/out procedure.
14. Instruct personnel in proper use of audio-visual equipment.	*I.L. 3%* *B.L. 1%*	All personnel who check out equipment shall demonstrate its use.	14.1	Create audio-visual use job aid.
15. Advise personnel on the selection and use of audio-visual courseware.	*I.L. 1%* *B.L. .5%*	Discuss potential uses for all available course-ware.	15.1	View all available courseware.
			15.2	Develop job aid of uses for all available courseware.
16. Answer telephone to take messages, furnish information, and obtain information.	*I.L. 7%* *B.L. 1%*	Direct all calls to appropriate information source.	16.1	Prerequisite skill for the job.
			16.2	Provide checklist of frequently requested information and answers.
17. Order specialized training materials (reference materials, course materials, and audio-visual materials).	*I.L. 6%* *B.L. 1%*	All orders filled out correctly and sent to the right source.	17.1	Check sample of completed orders.
			17.2	Produce job aid showing how to complete orders and where to send for various materials.

Figure 6.6 (Continued)

(continued from page 194)

and beginning level Training Support Specialist in charge of scheduling.

The Learning Objective Technique was the last one used. Condition 5.3 in the master plan for intermediate and beginning level Training Support Specialists (Figure 6.6) demonstrates how this was applied. Condition 5.3 states that audio-visual repair training is essential to correct performance of the task "Clean and Repair Audio-Visual Equipment." The condition of training was placed on this task because of the high costs associated with poor or incorrect maintenance. Using the Learning .Objective Technique, the analyst reviewed the maintenance documents provided with each piece of audio-visual equipment used in the training department. The following learning objectives were developed as a result of the review:

1. *Terminal Objective*
   - Given all required materials and equipment, clean and repair audio-visual equipment correctly to avoid major repairs.

2. *Enabling Objectives*
   - Given an Ektagraphic AF-3 Slide Projector, an ELH lamp replacement, and a camel hair brush, replace the lamp and clean the mirror correctly without damaging any part of the projector.
   - Given a Wollensak Visual Sync Cassette Recorder, cotton swab, alcohol, and dry lint-free cloth, correctly clean the heads and case without damaging any part of the recorder.
   - Given a 3M Overhead Projector, ENX lamp replacement, camel hair brush, and replacement fuse, replace the lamp and fuse, and clean the mirror without damaging any part of the projector.
   - Given a Kodak Pageant 16mm Projector, an EJL bulb replacement, a camel hair brush, and lens paper, replace the bulb, clean the lens, and clean the lens track without damaging any part of the projector.
   - From memory, describe the importance of using a camel hair brush to clean the mirror and lens.

3. *Entry Behaviors*
  * Basic manual dexterity
  * Ability to read instruction manuals
  * Organization skills

The Final Report

The final report organizes all of the data of the analysis. It is an essential document that minimally includes the following sections:
  * *Cover page* with analysis title, analysts' names, and publishing organization.
  * *Table of Contents* outlining the sections of the report and page numbers.
  * *Introduction* describing the background of the job position being analyzed and the need for the analysis as well as a review of the goals, objectives, and other sections included in the analysis contract.
  * *Methodology* describing the analysis techniques that were used and the specific steps that were followed. This section should include resumes of the master performers and a description of how they were selected.
  * *Results* describing the general recommendations for implementing the analysis data with the data which supports the recommendations. It is best if this section is formatted as a job aid requiring specific actions of the report users. This is done by transferring the conditions from the master plan to a planning and scheduling chart as shown in Figure 6.7.
  * *Detailed data* including all analysis technique data. Typical contents are master plans, position matrices, job aids, task inventories, and learning objectives.
  * *Appendices* containing miscellaneous documents, such as interview schedules, analysis questionnaires, glossaries, references, analyst resumes, and indices.

Chapter Summary

To do a complete analysis of a job, it is important to draw on several techniques because a single technique seldom provides sufficient data to improve performance fully. And improved performance, after all, is the real reason for analyzing a job.

ACTIONS REQUIRED	PLANNED SCHEDULE	DATE COMPLETE
1. Develop facilities scheduling log.		
2. Develop audio-visual equipment scheduling log.		
3. Develop transportation scheduling log.		
4. Develop checklist of things to do to schedule transportation.		
5. Develop courseware scheduling log.		
6. Develop audio-visual maintenance schedule.		
7. Develop job aid for cleaning and repairing audio-visual equipment.		
8. Develop audio-visual equipment repair training session.		
9. Develop job aid showing where to send various equipment for repair.		

Figure 6.7. Results Summary and Planning Chart.

It is usually best to select techniques which describe what the job is, how the job is done, how the job could be improved, and how to learn or acquire the job. Selecting techniques from each of these categories results in a more comprehensive and useful final report.

Different techniques, of course, are needed in different situations. As was mentioned, there is always some art involved in selecting the "right" techniques. The analyst who works at becoming expert gains an experiential advantage that makes the selection process easier. By recognizing the various factors in a workplace that affect performance, the expert analyst is able to cut through the organizational structure to focus on key issues. A good analyst senses the appropriate direction, categorizes appropriate techniques, and devises an action plan for the analysis. The goal of this book has been to provide a description of techniques and action skills for valid analysis.

References

Detailed Bibliography of Job and Task Analysis Literature

Abramson, T.C. *Job and Task Analysis in the Evaluation of Vocational Education Programs. Special Interest Paper.* ERIC Document ED 185 250, 1979.

Adde, E.N. *A Methodological Strategy for Identifying Similarities Among Jobs.* Washington, D.C. U.S. Office of Personnel Management, 1980.

Airasain, P.W. The Use of Hierarchies in the Analysis and Planning of Chemistry Instruction. *Science Education,* 1970, Vol. 54, No. 1, pp. 91-95.

Allison, C.E. Job and Task Analysis "A View From the Inside." *Proceedings of the Fourth Symposium on Training of Nuclear Facility Personnel.* Gatlinburg, TN: American Nuclear Society, 1981, April, pp. 27-28.

Ammerman, H.L., and Pratzner, F.C. *Performance Content for Job Training.* 5 Vols. Columbus, OH: Center for Vocational Education, Ohio State University, 1977.

Annett, J. and Duncan, K.D. Task Analysis: A Critique. In Barnes, J. and Robinson, N. (eds.), *New Media and Methods in Industrial Training.* London: British Broadcasting Corporation, 1968.

Annett, J. and Duncan, K.D. Task Analysis and Training Design. *Occupational Psychology,* 1975, Vol. 41, pp. 211-221.

Archer, W.B. *Computation of Group Job Descriptions from Occupational Survey Data.* No. PRL-TR-66-12. Lackland Air Force Base, TX: Personnel Research Laboratory, 1966.

Arvey, R.D., and Mossholer, K.M. A Proposed Methodology for Determining Similarities and Differences Among Jobs. *Personnel Psychology,* 1977, Vol. 3, No. 3, pp. 363-374.

Barnes, R.M. *Motion and Time Study Design and Measurement*, 7th ed. New York: John Wiley & Sons, 1980.

Berelson, B. Content Analysis. In Lindzey, G. (Ed.) *Handbook of Social Psychology, Vol. 1.* Reading, MA: Addison-Wesley, 1954.

Berkell, D.E. Psycho-Educational and Task-Analytical Models: A Conceptual Framework for Comparison. *Educational Technology*, 1982, September, pp. 28-29.

Bernard, M.E. *Task Analysis in Instructional Program Development.* Theoretical Paper No. 52, Wisconsin Research and Development Center for Cognitive Learning, University of Wisconsin. ERIC Document ED 114 735, 1975.

Bernhard, K., and DiPaolo, A. Profiling and Targeting Training and Development Needs. *NPSI Journal*, 1982, December, pp. 12-14.

Bloom, B.S. *Taxonomy of Educational Objectives, Handbook 1: Cognitive Domain.* New York: Longman, 1956.

Bobbitt, F. *How to Make a Curriculum.* Boston: Houghton Mifflin, 1924.

Borman, W.C., Dunnette, M.D., and Hough, L.M. *Development of Behaviorally Based Rating Scales for Evaluating the Performance of U.S. Navy Recruiters.* NPRDC TR-76-31. Minneapolis, MI: Personnel Decisions, Inc., 1976.

Bouchard, T.J. *A Manual for Job Analysis.* Minneapolis, MI: Minnesota Civil Service Department, 1972.

Boydell, T.H. *A Guide to Job Analysis.* London: British Association for Commercial and Industrial Education (BACIE), 1973.

Bradley, J. How to Interview for Information. *Training/HRD*, 1983, Vol. 20, No. 4, pp. 59-62.

Braune, R., and Foshay, W.R. Towards a Practical Model of Cognitive/Information Processing Task Analysis and Schema Acquisition for Complex Problem-Solving Situations. *Instructional Science*, 1983, Vol. 12, pp. 121-145.

Brightman, Harvey J. *Problem Solving: A Logical and Creative Approach.* Atlanta, GA: Business Publishing Division, College of Business, Georgia State University, 1980.

Bullock, D.H. Guiding Job Performance with Job Aids. *Training and Development Journal*, 1982, September, pp. 36-42.

Carlisle, K.E. *Towards a Methodology for Assessing Consistency Between Multiple Network Matrix Task Analyses of the Same Task.* Unpublished doctoral dissertation, Indiana University, 1981.

Carlisle, K.E. The Learning Strategy Technique of Task Analysis. *NPSI Journal*, 1982, Vol. 21, No. 10, pp. 9-11 & 41.

Carlisle, K.E. The Process of Task Analysis: Integrating Training's Multiple Methods. *Journal of Instructional Development*, 1983, Vol, 6, No. 4, pp. 31-35.

Carlisle, K.E. Improving Task Analysis in the Nuclear Utility Industry. *NPSI Journal*, 1983, Vol. 22, No. 2, pp. 8-9 & 27.

Carlisle, K.E. Three Techniques for Task Analysis: Examples from the Nuclear Utilities. *Performance and Instruction Journal*, 1984, Vol. 23, No. 3, pp. 13-16.

Carpenter, J.B. *Sensitivity of Group Job Descriptions to Possible Inaccuracies in Individual Job Descriptions.* No. AFHRL-TR-74-6. Brooks Air Force Base, TX: Air Force Human Resources Laboratory, 1974.

Carpenter, J.B., Biorgia, M.J., and McFarland , B.P. *Comparative Analysis of the Relative Validity for Subjective Time Rating Scales.* No. AFHRL-TR-75-63. Brooks Air Force Base, TX: Air Force Human Resources Laboratory, 1975.

Center for Vocational Education. *Directory of Task Inventories.* Vol. 1. Columbus, OH: Center for Vocational Education, Ohio State University, 1974.

Chane, G.W. *Motion and Time Study.* New York: Harper and Brothers, 1942.

Chapanis, A. *Man-Machine Engineering.* Belmont, CA: Wadsworth Publishing Co., 1965.

Chensoff, A., and Folley, J. *Guidelines for Training Situation Analysis.* Velensia, PA: Applied Science Associates, 1965.

Christal, R.E. *Stability of Consolidated Job Descriptions Based on Task Inventory Survey Information.* No. AFHRL-TR-71-48. Lackland Air Force Base, TX: Air Force Human Relations Laboratory, 1971.

Christal, R.E. *The United States Air Force Occupational Research Project.* No. AFHRL-TR-73-75. Brooks Air Force Base, TX: Air Force Human Resources Laboratory, 1974.

Clark, F. Improving Technical Skills in an Urban Transit Environment. *Training and Developmental Journal*, 1982, September, pp. 58-62.

Clary, J.N. *Naval Occupational Task Analysis Program Data Bank Information: Its Use in the Development/Updating or Qualifications for Advancement.* No. WTR-73-32. Washington, D.C.: Navel Personnel Research and Development Laboratory, 1973.

Close, G.C. *Word Improvement.* New York: John Wiley and Sons, 1960.

Coldeway, D.O., and Rasmussen, R.V. *Conducting Task Analysis: The Effects of Interpersonal Dynamics.* ERIC Document, ED 177 622, 1979.

Companion, M.A., and Teichner, W.H. *Application of Task Theory to Task Analysis: Evaluation of Validity and Reliability Using Simple Tasks.* Washington, D.C.: Air Force Office of Scientific Research (NL), Bolling AFB, 1977.

Cotterman, T.E. *Task Classification: An approach to Partially Ordering Information on Human Learning.* WADC-TN 58-374. Dayton, OH: Wright Air Development Center, 1959.

Cotton, J.W., Gallagher, J.P., and Marshall, S.P. The Identification and Decomposition of Hierarchical Tasks. *American Educational Research Journal*, 1977, Vol. 14, No. 3, pp. 189-212.

Cragun, J.R., and McCormick, E.J. *Job Inventory Information: Task and Scale Reliabilities and Scale Interrelationships.* No. PRL-TR-67-15. Lackland Air Force Base, TX: Personnel Research Laboratory, 1967.

Crossman, E.R.F.W. Perceptual Activities in Manual Work. *Research*, 1956, Vol. 9, p. 42.

Crystal, J.C., and Deems, R.S. Redesigning Jobs. *Training and Development Journal*, 1983, February, pp. 44-46.

Cunningham, D.J. Task Analysis and Part Versus Whole Learning Methods. *AVCR*, 1971, Vol. 19, No. 4, pp. 365-398.

Davies, I.K. The Analytical and Synthetic Stages of Programmed Writing. *Programmed Learning: The Journal of the Association for Programmed Learning and Educational Technology*, 1965, Vol. 2, No. 2.

Davies, I.K. *The Management of Learning.* London: McGraw-Hill, 1971.

Davies, I.K. Presentation Strategies. In Hartley, J. (Ed.), *Strategies for Programmed Instruction: An Educational Technology.* London: Butterworths, 1972.

Davies, I.K. Task Analysis: Some Process and Content Concerns. *AVCR*, 1973, Vol. 21, pp. 73-85.

Davies, I.K. *Competency Based Learning.* New York: McGraw-Hill Book Co., 1973.

Davies, I.K. *Objectives in Curriculum Design.* London: McGraw-Hill Book Co., 1976.

Davies, I.K. Task Analysis for Reliable Human Performance. *NPSI Journal*, 1981, Vol. 20, No. 2, pp. 8-10.

D'Costa, A.G., and Watson, J.E. A Critical-Incident Technique for Developing Criterion-Referenced Tests. *Educational Technology*, 1983, Vol. 23, No. 7, pp. 13-16.

DeBono, E. *Lateral Thinking.* New York: Penguin Books, 1977.

Deden-Parker, A. Needs Assessment in Depth: Professional Training at Wells Fargo Bank. *Journal of Instructional Development*, 1980, Vol. 1, No. 1, pp. 3-9.

Delp, P. *et al. Systems Tools for Project Planning.* Bloomington, IN: Program of Advanced Studies in Institution Building and Technical Assistance Methodology, 1977.

Diekhoff, G.M., and Diekhoff, K.B. Cognitive Maps as a Tool in Communicating Structural Knowledge. *Educational Technology*, 1981, Vol. 21, No. 4, pp. 28-30.

Drauden, G.M. and Peterson, N.G. Domain-Sampling Approach to Job Analysis. *JSAS Catalog of Selected Documents in Psychology*, 1977, Vol. 7, pp. 27-28.

Duncan, K. Strategies for Analysis of a Task. In Hartley, J. (Ed.), *Strategies for Programmed Instruction: An Educational Technology.* London: Butterworths, 1972.

Elstein, A., Shulman, L., and Sprafka, S. *Medical Problem-Solving.* Cambridge, MA: Harvard University Press, 1976.

Farrell, W.T., Stone, C.H., and Yoder, D. *Guidelines for Sampling in Marine Corps Task Analysis.* No. TR-11. Los Angeles, CA: California State University, 1976.

Fields, A. Getting Started: Pattern Notes and Perspectives. In Jonassen, D.H. (Ed.), *The Technology of Text: Principles for Structuring, Designing, and Displaying Text.* Englewood Cliffs, NJ: Educational Technology Publications, 1982.

Fine, S.A. Functional Job Analysis: An Approach to a Technology for Manpower Planning. *Personnel Journal,* 1974, November, pp. 813-818.

Fine, S.A., and Wiley, W.W. *An Introduction to Functional Job Analysis.* Kalamazoo, MI: W.E. Upjohn Institute for Employment Research, 1971.

Flanagan, J.C. Defining the Requirements of the Executive's Job. *Personnel,* 1951, Vol. 28, No. 1, pp. 28-35.

Flanagan, J.C. The Critical Incident Technique. *Psychological Bulletin,* 1954, Vol. 51, pp. 327-358.

Fleishman, E.A. Relating Individual Differences to the Dimensions of Human Tasks. *Ergonomics,* 1978, Vol. 21, No. 12, pp. 1007-1019.

Folley, J.D. *Development of an Improved Method of Task Analysis and Beginnings of a Theory of Training.* NAVTRADEVCEN, 1218-1. New York: U.S. Naval Training Device Center, 1964.

Foshay, W.R. Alternative Method of Task Analysis: A Comparison of Three Techniques. *Journal of Instructional Development,* 1983, Vol. 6, No. 4, pp. 2-10.

Freda, L.J., and Loolioan, J.K. Task Analysis as a Training Determinator: One Organization's Approch. *Educational Technology,* 1975, Vol. 15, No. 9, pp. 22-27.

Fugill, J.W.K. *Task Difficulty and Task Aptitude Benchmark Scales for the Administrative and General Career Fields.* No. AFHRL-73-13. Brooks Air Force Base, TX: Air Force Human Resources Laboratory, 1972.

Fugill, J.W.K. *Task Difficulty and Task Aptitude Benchmark Scales for the Mechanical and Electronics Career Fields.* No. AFHRL-TR-7240. Brooks Air Force Base, TX: Air Force Human Resources Laboratory, 1972.

Gael, S. *Job Analysis: A Guide to Assessing Work Activities.* San Francisco, CA: Jossey-Bass, Inc., 1983.

Gagné, R.M. Military Training and Principles of Learning. *American Psychologist,* 1962, Vol. 17.

Gagné, R.M. Learning Hierarchies. *Educational Psychologist,* 1968, Vol. 6, No. 1, pp. 3-6 & 9.

Gagné, R.M. Task Analysis: Its Relation to Content Analysis. *Educational Psychologist,* 1974, Vol. 2, No. 1, pp. 11-18.

Gagné, R.M. *The Conditions of Learning* (3rd ed.). New York: Holt, Rinehart, and Winston, 1977.

Gerlach, V.S., Reiser, R.A., and Brecke, P.H. Algorithms in Education. *Educational Technology,* 1977, October, pp. 14-18.

Gibbons, A.S. Task and Content Analysis Methods—An Expanding View. In

Schroeder, P.E. (Ed.), *Proceedings of a Symposium on Task Analysis/Task Inventories*. ERIC Document ED 126 314, 1975.

Gibbons, A.S. *A Review of Content and Task Analysis Methodology*, (Tech. Rep. No. 2, Courseware, Inc.), ERIC Document Ed 143 696, 1977.

Gibbons, A.S. Pre-development Analysis in Military Training. *NPSI Journal*, 1980, Vol. 19, No. 1, pp. 34-42.

Gilbert, A.C.F. *Dimensions of Certain Army Officer Positions Derived by Factor Analysis*. No. ARI-TP-269. Arlington, VA: Army Research Institute for the Behavioral and Social Sciences, 1975.

Gilbert, T.F. Mathetics: The Theory of Education. *Journal of Mathetics*, 1962, Vol. 1, No. 1, pp. 7-73.

Gilbert, T.F. Praxeonomy: A Systematic Approach to Identifying Training Needs. *Management of Personnel Quarterly*, 1967, Vol. 6, No. 3.

Gilbert, T.F. *Human Competence: Engineering Worthy Performance.* New York: McGraw-Hill Book, 1978.

Gilbert, T.F. Measuring Potential for Performance Improvement. *Training/HRD*, 1978, December.

Gilbert, T.F. Guiding Worthy Performance. *Improving Human Performance Quarterly*, 1978, Vol. 7, No. 3, pp. 273-302.

Gilbert, T.F. Analyzing Productive Performance. In Fredericksen, L.W. (Ed.), *Handbook of Organizational Behavior Management.* New York: John Wiley and Sons, 1982.

Gilbert, T.F. A Question of Performance—Part I: The PROBE Model. *Training and Development Journal*, 1982, Vol. 36, No. 9, pp. 21-30.

Gilbert, T.F. A Question of Performance—Part II: Applying the PROBE Model. *Training and Development Journal*, 1982, Vol. 36, No. 10, pp. 85-89.

Gilbreth, F.B. *Brick Laying System.* New York: Clark Publishing, 1911.

Gilpatrick, E. and Gullion, C. *The Health Service Mobility Study Method of Task Analysis and Curriculum Design.* Research Report No. 1. 4 Vols. Washington, D.C.: Office of Research and Development, 1977.

Grossman, S.R. Brainstorming Updated. *Training and Development Journal*, 1984, February, pp. 84-87.

Guided Design Newsletter. Morgantown, WV: Guided Design Center, Engineering Sciences Building, West Virginia University.

Hale, J.R. Occupational, Job, and Task Analysis: Tools for Trainers and Personnel Specialists. *Personnel Selection and Training Bulletin*, 1981, Vol. 1, No. 2.

Handbook for Analyzing Jobs. U.S. Department of Labor, Manpower Administration, Washington, D.C.: U.S. Government Printing Office (Stock No. 2900-0131), 1972.

Hannum, W.H. Toward a Framework for Task Analysis. *Educational Technology*, 1974, Vol. 14, No. 2, pp. 57-58.

Hannum, W.H. Task Analysis Procedures. *NPSI Journal*, 1980, Vol. 19, No. 3, pp. 6-7, 14.

Hansen, B.L. *Work Sampling for Modern Management.* Englewood Cliffs, NJ: Prentice-Hall, 1960.

Harless, J.H. *An Ounce of Analysis (Is Worth a Pound of Programming).* Washington, D.C.: Harless Performance Guild, Inc., 1971.

Harless, J.H. Task Analysis: A Clarification of the Term. *NPSI Journal,* 1980, Vol. 19, No. 1, pp. 4-5.

Harmon, P. The Design of Instructional Materials: A Top-Down Approach. *Journal of Instructional Development,* 1982, Vol. 6, No. 1, pp. 6-14.

Harmon, P.H. Task Analysis: A Top-Down Approach. *Performance and Instruction Journal,* 1983, May, pp. 14-19.

Hartley, J., and Davies, I.K. *Contributions to an Educational Technology,* Vol. 2. London: Kogan Page, 1979.

Heiland, R.F., and Richardson, W.J. *Work Sampling.* New York: McGraw-Hill, 1957.

Hemphill, J.K. Job Descriptions for Executives. *Harvard Business Review,* 1959, Vol. 37, pp. 55-67.

Hershback, D.R. Deriving Instructional Content Through Task Analysis. *Journal of Industrial Teacher Education,* 1976, Vol. 13, No. 3, pp. 63-73.

Hershback, D.R. Selection and Differentiation of Instructional Tasks. *Journal of Industrial Teacher Education,* 1977, Vol. 14, No. 3, pp. 7-18.

Hoffman, C.K., and Medsker, K.L. Instructional Analysis: The Missing Link Between Task Analysis and Objectives. *Journal of Instructional Development, 1983, Vol. 6, No. 4, pp. 17-24.*

Institute of Nuclear Power Operations. *Task Analysis Procedure, INPO 83-009.* Atlanta, GA: Author, 1983.

Jackson, S.F., and Bullock, D.H. Job Analysis. *The Training Consultants' Memo,* 1983, Vol. 2, No. 8-9, pp. 1-14.

Janson, R. Developing a Motivational Strategy. *Training and Development Journal,* 1979, Vol. 33, No. 9, pp. 56-65.

Janson, R. Work Redesign: A Results-Oriented Strategy That Works. *S.A.M. Advanced Management Journal,* 1979, Vol. 44, No. 1, pp. 21-27.

Jones, J.J., Jr., and DeCoths, T.A. Job Analysis: National Survey Findings. *Personnel Journal,* 1969, Vol. 49, pp. 805-809.

Jones, S. Why Can't Leaflets Be Logical? *New Society,* 1964, Vol. 102, p. 16.

Kaufman, R., and Mitchell, D.L. Risk and Training. *NPSI Journal,* 1982, March, pp. 4-7.

Kazarian, E.A. *Work Analysis and Design for Hotels, Restaurants and Institutions.* Westport, CT: The AVI Publishing Co., Inc., 1969.

Kepner-Tregoe, Inc. *Problem Analysis and Decision Making.* Princeton, NJ: Author, 1979.

Kepner, C.H., and Tregoe, B.B. *The New Rational Manager.* Princeton, NJ: Kepner-Tregoe, Inc., 1981.

Kennedy, P., Esque, T., and Novak, J. A Functional Analysis of Task Analysis Procedures for Instructional Design. *Journal of Instructional Development,* 1983, Vol. 6, No. 4, pp. 10-16.

Kershner, A.M. *A Report on Job Analysis.* USN, ONR Report ACR-5. Washington, D.C.: 1955.

King Taylor, L. *Not for Bread Alone: An Appreciation of Job Enrichment.* London: Business Books, 1973.

Kishi, A., and Stone, C.H. *Task Inventory Construction.* No. TR-14. Los Angeles, CA: California State University, 1976.

Koym, K.G. *Familiarity Effects on Task Difficulty Ratings.* No. AFHRL-TR-77-25. Brooks Air Force Base, TX: Air Force Human Resources Laboratory, 1977.

Koym, K.G. *Predicting Job Difficulty in High-Aptitude Career Ladders with Standard Score Regression Equations.* No. AFHRL-TR-77-26. Brooks Air Force Base, TX: Air Force Human Resources Laboratory, 1977.

Krathwohl, D.R., Bloom, B.S., and Masia, B.B. *Taxonomy of Educational Objectives, Handbook 2: Affective Domain.* New York: Longman, 1964.

Kuriloff, A.H., Yoder, D., and Stone, C.H. *Training Guide for Observing and Interviewing in Marine Corps Task Analysis.* Evaluation of the Marine Corps Task Analysis Program. Technical Report No. 2. Los Angeles, CA: California State University, 1975.

Landa, L.N. *Algorithmization in Learning and Instruction.* Englewood Cliffs, NJ: Educational Technology Publications, 1974.

Landa, L.N. *Instructional Regulation and Control: Cybernetics, Algorithmization, and Heuristics in Education.* Englewood Cliffs, NJ: Educational Technology Publications, 1976.

Landa, L.N. The Improvement of Instruction, Learning, and Performance. *Educational Technology*, 1982, Vol. 22, No. 10, pp. 7-12.

Latham, G.P. Behavior-Based Assessment for Organizations. In Frederiksen, L.W. (Ed.), *Handbook of Organizational Behavior Management.* New York: John Wiley and Sons, 1982.

Latterner, C.G. Task Analysis: Bane or Blessing? In Ofiesh, G.D , and Meierhenry, W.C. (Eds.), *Trends in Programmed Instruction.* Washington, D.C.: Department of Audio-Visual Instruction, National Education Association, 1964.

Lawson, T.E. Gagne's Learning Theory Applied to Technical Instruction. *Training and Development Journal*, 1974, April, pp. 32-40.

Lehrer, R.N. *Work Simplification: Creative Thinking About Work Problems.* Englewood Cliffs, NJ: Prentice-Hall, 1957.

Lesperance, J.P. *Economics and Techniques of Motion and Time Study.* Dubuque, Iowa: Wm. C. Brown Co., 1954.

Lewis, B.T., and Pearson, W.W. *Management Guide for Work Simplification.* New York: John F. Rider Pub., 1961.

Lewis, L. Job Analysis in the United States Training and Employment Service. In *Proceedings of Division of Military Psychology Symposium*, pp. 23-41, 77th Annual Convention of the American Psychological Association, USAF, AFPTRC, Personnel Research Division, Lackland AFB, TX: 1969.

Lineberry, C.S. When to Develop Aids for On-the-Job Use and When to Provide Instruction. *Improving Human Performance Quarterly*, 1977, Vol. 6, No. 2, pp. 87-92.

Lineberry, C.S., and Bullock, D.H. *Job Aids*. Englewood Cliffs, NJ: Educational Technology Publications, 1980.

Madden, J.M., Hazel, J.T., and Christal, R.E. *Worker and Supervisor Agreement Concerning the Worker's Job Description*. No. PRL-TDR-64-10. Lackland Air Force Base, TX: Aerospace Medical Division, 1964.

Mager, R.F. *Preparing Instructional Objectives*. Belmont, CA: Fearon/Pitman, 1962.

Mager, R.F., and Beach, K.M. *Developing Vocational Instruction*. Belmont, CA: Fearon/Pitman, 1967.

Mager, R.F., and Pipe, P. *Analyzing Performance Problems or "You Really Oughta Wanna"*. Belmont, CA: Fearon/Pitman, 1970.

Mager, R.F. *Goal Analysis*. Belmont, CA: Fearon/Pitman, 1972.

Mager, R.F. *Measuring Instructional Intent: Or Got A Match*. Belmont, CA: Fearon/Pitman, 1973.

Mallory, W.J. A Task-Analytic Approach to Specifying Technical Training Needs. *Training and Development Journal*, 1982, September, pp. 66-73.

Mangin, A.M. Job and Task Analysis for Instructional Development in the Nuclear Power Industry. *Proceedings of the Fourth Symposium on Training of Nuclear Facility Personnel*. Gatlinburg, TN: April 27-29, 1981.

Markowitz, J. Four Methods of Job Analysis. *Training and Development Journal*, 1981, September, pp. 112-118.

Marshall, C.T. *Occupational Analysis: Transition of the Navy Occupational Task Analysis Program (NOTAP) from Research to Operational Status– Evaluation of Program and Summation of Results*. No. WTR-73-37. Washington, D.C.: Navy Personnel Research and Development Center, 1973.

Martin, M.C., and Brodt, D.E. Task Analysis for Training and Curriculum Design. *Improving Human Performance: A Research Quarterly*, 1973, Vol. 2, p. 113-120.

Maynard, H.B., Stegemerten, G.J., and Schwab, J.L. *Methods Time Measurement*. New York: McGraw-Hill Book Co., 1962.

Mayo, C.C. *Three Studies of Job Inventory Procedures: Selecting Duty Categories, Interviewing, and Sampling*. No AFHRL-TR-69-32. Brooks Air Force Base, TX: Air Force Human Resources Laboratory, 1969.

Mayo, C.C., Nance, D.M., and Shigekawa, L. *Evaluation of the Job Inventory Approach Analyzing USAF Officer Utilization Fields*. No. AFHRL-TR-75-22. Brooks Air Force Base, TX: Air Force Human Resources Laboratory, 1975.

McCormick, E.J. *Effect of Amount of Information Required on Reliability of Incumbents' Checklist Reports*. No. WADD-TN-60-142. Lackland Air Force Base, TX: Personnel Laboratory, Wright Air Development Division, 1960.

McCormick, E.J. Job Analysis: An Overview. *Indian Journal of Industrial Relations*, 1970, July, pp. 5-14.

McCormick, E.J. *Job Analysis: Methods and Applications.* New York: AMACOM, a Division of American Management Association, 1979.

McCormick, E.J., and Ammerman, H.L. *Development of Worker Activity Checklists for Use in Occupational Analysis.* No. WADD-TR-60-77. Lackland Air Force Base, TX: Personnel Laboratory, Wright Air Development Division, 1960.

McCormick, E.J., Jeanneret, P.R., and Mecham, R.C. A Study of Job Characteristics and Job Dimensions as Based on the Position Analysis Questionnaire (PAQ). *Journal of Applied Psychology*, 1972, Vol. 56, pp. 347-368.

McCormick, E.J., and Tombrink, K.B. *A Comparison of Three Types of Work Activity Statements in Terms of Consistency of Job Information Reported by Incumbents.* No. WADD-TR-60-80. Lackland Air Force Base, TX: Personnel Laboratory, Wright Air Development Division, 1960.

McDermott, F.M. Try Brainstorming: A Quick Route to Job Analysis. *Training/HRD*, 1982, Vol. 19, No. 3, pp. 39-40.

Mead, D.F. *Continuation Study on Development of a Method for Evaluating Job Difficulty.* No. AFHRL-TR-70-43. Lackland Air Force Base, TX: Air Force Human Resources Laboratory, 1970.

Mead, D.F. *Development of an Equation for Evaluating Job Difficulty.* No. AFHRL-TR-70-42. Lackland Air Force Base, TX: Air Force Human Resources Laboratory, 1970.

Mead, D.F., and Christal, R.E. *Development of a Constant Standard Weight Equation for Evaluating Job Difficulty.* No. AFHRL-TR-70-44. Lackland Air Force Base, TX: Air Force Human Resources Laboratory, 1970.

Melching, W.H., and Borcher, S.D. *Procedures for Constructing and Using Task Inventories.* Center for Vocational and Technical Education, Research and Development Series No. 91. Columbus, Ohio: The Ohio State University, 1973.

Merrill, M.D. Structures of Task Analysis. *AVCR*, 1973, No. 1, p. 21.

Merrill, M.D. Content and Instructional Analysis for Cognitive Transfer Tasks. *AVCR*, 1973, Vol. 21, No. 1, pp. 109-125.

Merrill, M.D., and Tennyson, R.D. *Teaching Concepts: An Instructional Design Guide.* Englewood Cliffs, NJ: Educational Technology Publications, 1977.

Merrill, P.F. Task Analysis: An Information Processing Approach. *NPSI Journal*, 1976, Vol. 15, No. 2, pp. 7-11.

Merrill, P.F. Hierarchical and Information Processing Task Analysis: A Comparison. *Journal of Instructional Development*, 1978, Vol. 1, No. 2, pp. 35-40.

Merrill, P.F. Analysis of a Procedural Task. *NPSI Journal*, Vol. 19, No. 1, pp. 11-15 & 26.

Merrill, P.F. Representations for Algorithms. *NPSI Journal*, 1980, Vol. 19, No. 8, pp. 18-24.

Milbourn, G. A Primer on Implementing Job Redesign. *Supervisory Management*, 1981, Vol. 26, No. 1, pp. 27-37.

Miller, R.B. *A Method for Man-Machine Task Analysis.* TR 53-137. Dayton, OH: Wright-Patterson AFB, 1953.

Miller, R.B. *A Suggested Guide to Position Task Description* (Technical Memorandum ASPR-TM-56-6). Lackland Air Force Base, TX: Air Force Personnel and Training Research Center, 1956.

Miller, R. Task Description and Analysis. In Gagné, R.M. (Ed.), *Psychological Principles in System Development.* New York: Holt, Rinehart, and Winston, 1962.

Mooney, W.L. Other Applications for Job/Task Analysis in the Nuclear Electric Industry. *Personnel Selection and Training Bulletin*, 1982, Vol. 3, No. 2, pp. 105-108.

Morsh, J.E., and Archer, W.B. *Procedural Guide for Conducting Occupational Surveys in the United States Air Force.* USAF, AMD, Personnel Research Laboratory, PRL-TR-67-11, AD-664-036. Lackland AFB, TX: 1967.

Morsh, J.E., and Christal, R.E. *Impact of the Computer on Job Analysis in the United States Air Force.* USAF Personnel Research Laboratory, TR-66-19. Lackland AFB, TX: 1966.

Morsh, J.E., Madden, J.M., and Christal, R.E. *Job Analysis in the United States Air Force.* No. WADD-TR-61-113. Lackland Air Force Base, TX: Personnel Laboratory, Wright Air Development Division, 1961.

Mundel, M.E. *Motion and Time Study*, 4th ed. Englewood Cliffs, N.J.: Prentice-Hall, 1970.

Murray-Hicks, M. Analysis Techniques for Management Skills. *NPSI Journal*, 1981, May, pp. 16-20.

Nadler, G. *Motion and Time Study.* New York: McGraw-Hill Book Co., 1955.

Nadler, G. *Work Simplification.* New York: McGraw-Hill Book Co., 1957.

Nadler, G. *Work Design.* Homewood, IL: Richard D. Irwin, 1963.

Nelson, E.C., Jacobs, A.R., and Breer, P.E. Study of the Validity of Task Inventory Method of Job Analysis. *Medical Care*, 1975, Vol. 13, pp. 104-113.

Niebel, B.W. *Motion and Time Study.* Homewood, IL: Richard D. Irwin, 1962.

Pass, J.J., and Robertson, D.W. *Methods to Evaluate Scales and Sample Size for Stable Task Inventory Information.* No. NPRDC-TR-80-28. San Diego, CA: Navy Personnel Research and Development Center, 1980.

Patrick, J., and Stammers, R. Analysis for Training. In Hartley, J., and Davies, I.K. (Eds.), *Contribution to an Educational Technology*, Vol. 2. London: Kogan Page, 1978.

Paul, W.J., and Robertson, K.B. *Job Enrichment and Employee Motivation.* Epping, UK: Grower Press, 1970.

Peterson, R.O., and Duffany, B.H. Job Enrichment and Redesign. In Craig, R.L. (Ed.), *Training and Development Handbook.* New York: McGraw-Hill, 1976, pp. 15.1-15.15.

Porta, M.M. Job Performance Aids as Tools for Learning. *NSPI Journal*, 1979, Vol. 18, No. 10.

Prien, E.P. and Ronan, W.W. Job Analysis: A Review of Research Funding. *Personnel Psychology*, 1971, Vol. 24, pp. 371-396.

Rackham, N., and Morgan, T. *Behavior Analysis in Training.* London: McGraw-Hill, 1977.

Reason, J. Skill and Error in Everyday Life. In Howe, J.J.A. (Ed.), *Adult Learning: Psychology Research and Applications.* New York: John Wiley and Sons, 1977.

Reigeluth, C.M. Current Trends in Task Analysis: The Integration of Task Analysis and Instructional Design. *Journal of Instructional Development*, 1983, Vol. 6, No. 4, pp. 24-30.

Reigeluth, C.M., Merrill, M.D., and Bunderson, C.V. The Structure of Subject Matter Content and Its Instructional Design Implications. *Instructional Science*, 1978, Vol. 7, pp. 107-126.

Reigeluth, C.M., Merrill, M., Wilson, B., and Spillner, R. The Elaboration Theory of Instruction: A Model for Sequencing and Synthesizing Instruction. *Instructional Science*, 1980, Vol. 9, No. 3, pp. 125-219.

Reigeluth, C.M., and Darwazeh, A. The Elaboration Theory's Procedure for Designing Instruction: A Conceptual Approach. *Journal of Instructional Development*, 1982, Vol. 5, No. 3, pp. 22-32.

Reigeluth, C.M., and Rodgers, C.A. The Elaboration Theory of Instruction. In Reigeluth, C.M. (Ed.), *Instructional Design Theories and Models: An Overview of Their Current Status.* Hillsdale, NJ: Lawrence Erlbaum Associates, 1983.

Resnick, L.B. Task Analysis in Instructional Design: Some Cases from Mathematics. In Klahr, D. (Ed.), *Cognition and Instruction.* New York: John Wiley and Sons, 1976.

Resnick, L.B., and Ford, W.W. The Analysis of Tasks for Instruction: An Information-Processing Approach. In Brigham, T.A. and Catania, A.C. (Eds.), *Handbook of Applied Behavior Analysis: Social and Instructional Processes.* New York: Irvington Publishers, 1982.

Resnick, L.B., Wang, M.C., and Kaplan, J. Task Analysis in Curriculum Design: A Hierarchically Sequenced Introductory Mathematics Curriculum. *Journal of Applied Behavior Analysis*, 1973, Vol. 6, No. 4, pp. 679-710.

Robinson, A.D. What You See Is What You Get. *Training and Development Journal*, 1984, May, pp. 34-39.

Romiszowski, A.J. *Designing Instructional Systems.* London: Kogan Page, 1981.

Romiszowski, A.J. A New Approach to the Analysis of Knowledge and Skills. In Winterburn, R., and Evans, L. (Eds.), *Aspects of Educational Technology XIV.* London: Kogan Page, 1980.

Ross, K.C. The Use of Task Analysis in Control Room Evaluations. *Proceedings of the Fourth Symposium on Training of Nuclear Facility Personnel.* Gatlinburg, TN: 1981, April 27-29, pp. 164-174.

Scandura, J. *Problem Solving*. New York: Academic Press, 1976.

Schroeder, P.E. (Ed.) *Proceedings of a Symposium on Task Analyses/Task Inventories*. Columbus, OH: Center for Vocational Education, Ohio State University, 1975.

Seymour, W. *Industrial Skills*. London: Pitman, 1966.

Seymour, W. *Skills Analysis Training*. London: Pitman, 1968.

Shepard, A. An Improved Tabular Format for Task Analysis. *Journal of Occupational Psychology*, 1976, Vol. 49, pp. 93-104.

Sherman, T.M., and Wildman, T.M. *Linking Task Analysis with Student Learning*. ERIC Document ED 195 229.

Sherill, J.L. Analysis Approaches in Instructional Design. *Educational Technology*, 1972, Vol. 12, No. 8, pp. 42-45.

Shevlin, J.D. *Time Study and Motion Economy for Supervisors*. Chicago: National Foremen's Institute, Inc., 1945.

Siegel, A.I., Bartter, W.D., and Kopstein, F.F. *Job Analysis for Maintenance Mechanics in Nuclear Power Plants*. Wayne, PA: Applied Psychological Services, 1981.

Siegler, R.S. Recent Trends in the Study of Cognitive Development: Variations on a Task Analytic Time. *Human Development*, 1980, Vol. 23, No. 4, pp. 278-285.

Simpson, E.J. *The Classification of Educational Objectives, Psychomotor Domain*. Urbana, Illinois: University of Illinois, BR 5-0090, ERD 251, 1966.

Solomon, G., and Bouloutian, A. Build a Performance System—Not a Training System. *Training and Development Journal*, 1982, September, pp. 32-34.

Snyder, M.B. Methods of Recording and Reporting Task Analysis Information. In *Uses of Task Analysis in Deriving Training and Training Equipment Requirements*, pp. 11-31. USAF, WADD, TR 60-593. Wright Patterson AFB, OH: 1960.

Spitzer, D. Try Fault Tree Analysis, a Step-By-Step Way to Improve Organizational Development. *Training/HRD*, 1980, February, pp. 58-69.

Stacy, W.J., and Hazel, J.T. *A Method of Determining Desirable Task Experiences for First-Line Supervisors*. No. AFHRL-TR-75-23. Brooks Air Force Base, TX: Air Force Human Resources Laboratory, 1975.

Stainer, F.W. Training for Fault Diagnosis. *Proceedings of the Institute of Electrical Engineers*, 1967, p. 114.

Stephens, K.G. *A Fault Tree Approach to Analysis of Educational Systems as Demonstrated in Vocational Education*. Unpublished Doctoral Dissertation, University of Washington, 1972.

Stone, C.H. *Evaluation of the Marine Corps Task Analysis Program*. No. TR-16. Los Angeles, CA: California State University, 1976.

Stone, C.H., and Yoder, D. *Job Analysis 1970*. Long Beach, CA: California State College, 1970.

Student Print Material for the U.S. Air Force Course System, Instructional System Designer, Second Edition, Book 3. Reproduced and Distributed by the National Laboratory for the Advancement of Education. C/O Aerospace Education Foundation, 1750 Pennsylvania Avenue, NW, Washington, DC 20006.

Sullivan, H.S. Developing Objectives-Based Instruction. *Educational Technology*, 1971, July, Vol. 11, No. 7, pp. 55-57.

Swann, J.H. *Interpretation and Training Uses of Computer Printout Data of Naval Occupational Task Analysis Program* (NOTAP). No. WTR-73-34. Washington, D.C.: Naval Personnel Research and Development Laboratory, 1973.

Task Analysis Inventories. U.S. Department of Labor, Manpower Administration. Washington, D.C.: U.S. Government Printing Office (Stock No. 2900-00163), 1973.

Task Analysis: Training's Enduring Workhorse. *Training/HRD*, 1982, February, pp. 80-83.

Taylor, F.W. *Principles of Scientific Management.* New York: Harper & Row, 1947.

Terrel, W.R. Algorithmic Processes for Increasing Design Efficiency. *Journal of Instructional Development*, 1983, Vol. 6, No. 2, pp. 33-41.

Terry, D.R., and Evans, R.N. *Methodological Study for Determining the Task Content of Dental Auxiliary Education Programs.* No. HRP 000-4628. Bethesda, MD: Bureau of Health Manpower Education, National Institutes of Health, 1973.

Thornley, D.H., and Valentine, G.A. Job Enlargement: Some Implications of Longer Cycle Jobs on Fan Heater Production. *Philips Personnel Management Review*, 1968.

Tiemann, P., and Markle, S. *Analyzing Instructional Content: A Guide to Instruction and Evaluation.* Champaign, IL: Stipes Publishing Co., 1978.

Trattner, M.H. Task Analysis in the Design of Three Concurrent Validity Studies of the Professional and Administrative Career Examination. *Personnel Psychology*, 1979, Vol. 32, pp. 109-119.

Utt, C.T. Flow-Process Charts: How They Help Determine Employee Training Needs. *Training/HRD*, 1982, January, pp. 80-81.

Van Gundy, A.B. *Techniques of Structured Problem Solving.* New York: Van Nostrand-Reinhold, 1981.

Walter, S., and Earle, R.S. Contracting for Instructional Development. *Journal of Instructional Development*, 1981-82, Vol. 5, No. 2, pp. 26-31.

Willis, J.L. Nuclear Power Plant Operator Task and Skills Analysis: A Call for Innovation. *Proceedings of the Fourth Symposium on Training of Nuclear Facility Personnel.* Gatlinburg, TN: 1981, April 27-29.

Wilson, A., and Goodman, R.L. Task-Unit Scheduling for Improved Service and Productivity. *The Cornell H.R.A. Quarterly*, 1984, August, pp. 78-83.

Wyant, T.G. Syllabus Analysis. In Budgett, R. and Leedham, J. (Eds.), *Aspects of Educational Technology VI.* London: Pitman, 1973.

Wyant, T.G. Network Analysis. In Howe, A., and Romiszowski, A.J. (Eds.), *APLET Yearbook of Educational and Instructional Technology, 1974/75.* London: Pitman, 1974.

Yaney, J.P. A Critical Review of the Instructional Technology Mechanism of Task Analysis. *Improving Human Performance: A Research Quarterly*, 1974, Vol. 3, No. 2, pp. 64-70.

Zemke, R. Figuring Out What People Need to Learn. *Training/HRD*, 1977, December.

Zemke, R. The Critical Incident Method of Analysis. *Training/HRD*, 1979, April.

Zemke, R. Behavioral Observations: Why the 'Count and Chart' Approach to Task Analysis Pays Off. *Training/HRD*, 1979, Sept, pp. 90-93.

Zemke, R., and Kramlinger, T. *Figuring Things Out: A Trainer's Guide to Needs and Task Analysis.* Reading, MA: Addison-Wesley, 1982.

Zerga, J.E. Job Analysis: A Resume and Bibliography. *Journal of Applied Psychology*, 1943, Vol. 27, pp. 249-267.

Index